Celluloid Collectibles

IDENTIFICATION & VALUE GUIDE

Shirley Dunn

COLLECTOR BOOKS
A Division of Schroeder Publishing Co., Inc.

Dedication

In loving memory of my father and tribute to my mother who both encouraged me with their unconditional love to excel in whatever I wished to do and gave me the courage to succeed.

Searching for a Publisher?

We are always looking for knowledgeable people considered to be experts within their fields. If you feel that there is a real need for a book on your collectible subject and have a large comprehensive collection, contact Collector Books.

Printed by IMAGE GRAPHICS, INC., Paducah, Kentucky

Acknowledgments

A true friend is there when you need them in happiness and travail. The ‌elopment and conception of this book began after a 25 year collection process ‌a relatively long courtship. Much of that time, my neighbor and friend Jean ‌lottmann often shopped with me and encouraged me to purchase those special ‌ns, often when I thought they were beyond my budget. She has even been ‌wn to say if you don't but this I'll never shop with you again! And of course I ‌s always glad that I'd purchased that special item or it would have joined the ‌e that got away club."

Another special friend took the time to read from cover to cover — when ‌re weren't yet covers. And what do you know, Ginny? My editor agreed and ‌rranged the text as you suggested! Thanks to Virginia Miller for taking the time ‌get acquainted with my baby. Even the members of my bell choir showed an ‌erest as week after week the body of pictures grew.

But the person who went over word by word from beginning to end was my ‌ther. Just as I was there when she had her baby girl my sister, she is there for ‌ as she has been every day of my life. Thanks, Mom.

One dealer stands out as especially helpful throughout this gestation period. ‌every show she was there to encourage me and generously share her knowledge ‌h me, so a special thanks to Kathleen (Kitty) Victor of Blue Goose Antiques, ‌llevue, Washington.

Although I've yet to meet this lady, Andra Behrendt always had time to ‌pond to my telephone calls and letters. If it weren't for her, I would yet be ‌rching for a catalog from years ago. Courtesy of Andra I can share with you the ‌30 – 1931 du Pont catalog on pgs. 71 – 74 from her personal collection. She is an ‌thority and collector of celluloid covered boxes.

My ongoing special thanks goes to the man at my side for 42 years, my hus‌nd, Charles. He has been there throughout this birthing experience. He was ‌aware of the earlier effort of collecting for a decade or so, but in the end he has ‌come a good scout, as well as co-driver and photography information source. In ‌t, I think he has really gotten interested in this project as delivery date nears. ‌rhaps it is the anticipation of having things back to normal whatever that is!

I do need to mention one other person who shared his skills with me at the ‌rly photo sessions. It was a pleasure working with a professional, David Stein, in ‌e David Stein Professional Photography Studio. Please take special note of the ‌ger groups of items he photographed for me on pages 35, 76, 111, 113, 117, 118, ‌d 120. He helped me see my collection in another light.

All of the items in this book are from my personal collection with one excep‌n. I wish to thank Roy and Betty Barnes for allowing my husband and me to ‌it their home in Bingen, Washington, where I photographed the lovely peach-‌lored complete dresser set in the original fitted box. This dresser set had ‌longed to Betty's grandmother Margret Risley of Springfield, Pennsylvania.

With the competent efforts of the Collector Book staff the delivery will be ‌mplete. I hope you, the reader, will enjoy each item as much as I continue to do.

ABOUT THE AUTHOR

Shirley Morrison Dunn was born at 9 a.m. in early October of 1932. As the oldest child of Kester and Beulah Morrison, she grew up on a farm in the Kittitas Valley with grandparents and great-grandparents and cousins in nearby homes. Later a brother and sister joined the family in this small community in central Washington.

Shirley tried the usual farm girl delights of climbing trees and horseback riding with chores of feeding the chickens, ducks, and rabbits, and helping milk the cows. She picked strawberries and corn. Her special delight was bouncing across the hay fields with her mother on errands for the hay baling crew owned and run by her father.

While still attending Thorp High School, she developed an interest in journalism wrote the local column for the Ellensburg Record, later acquired as part of the Gan family. A recipient of the Smyser Scholarship, she took prerequisite classes at Cen Washington College and then received a Bachelor of Science in Occupational Ther with a psychology major from the University of Puget Sound, Tacoma, WA. It was at University that she met and married Charles Robert Dunn of Olympia, WA.

After establishing the first Occupational Therapy Dept. at St. Joseph's Hospita Tacoma, it was time for a family. With sons Robert and Richard, the move was made to family homestead on Cooper Point near Olympia, WA. where all could enjoy the view water of the southernmost tip of Puget Sound at their doorstep, as well as participate water skiing and boating.

As Shirley's family worked together in her childhood, so did the Dunn family w together in installing, maintaining, and monitoring security systems in a company foun by Charles Dunn and named Capitol Alarm for the nearby capitol city.

As a child Shirley had received a dresser set made of "French Ivory" from her ma nal grandmother. Perhaps this was the spark that later ignited into her intense interes this subject.

From the 1970s on, Shirley's membership in the Zonta Club of Olympia, an inter tional service organization, also gave her the opportunity to survey the collectible marke various locations from California to Canada and Chicago to Copenhagen.

Besides being president and manager of Capitol Alarm Inc., and holding vari offices in Zonta International on the local, district, and international level, Shirley is als member of United Churches of Olympia handbell choir, the American Association of U versity Women, a volunteer for the Easter Seal Society, and a "lamplighter" for U.S. Cc Guard, Dist.13 for nine years.

lls. He won the prize with a material composed of a mixture of paper ck, shellac, and collodion. Collodion (q.v.), patented in 1870 and regis- ed as a trademark by Hyatt, was a mixture of nitro cellulose, camphor, d a little alcohol. He found that the mixture was soft enough to mold der mild heat and pressure, but when cooled it became hard." Other omplishments were also listed.

At the request of John Carbutt, a Philadelphia maker of photographic tes, in 1888 Hyatt produced clear sheets of celluloid of thin uniform ckness suitable for a photographic base to replace the heavy and fragile ss plates then in use.

John Wesley Hyatt invented a widely used water purification filter; he vented and marketed the Hyatt roller bearing used in modern machines. I uld say the title American inventor was well deserved.

You probably have heard of other inventors of "celluloid." One seldom entioned is Alexander Parkes, born Dec. 29, 1813, Birmingham, Warwick- ire, England, died June 29, 1890, near London. He was a British chemist d inventor noted for his development of various industrial processes and aterials. Among his other accomplishments was producing a flexible, rable material called Parkesine (c. 1855) from a mixture of chloroform and stor oil that led to the development of the first plastic, celluloid (q.v.). nce some of my pieces are marked "England" I was sure that someone ust have been involved in similar production in England near the same riod of time.

According to Andrea DiNoto's *Art Plastic*, the so-called Celluloid era ted from 1880s to 1920s producing an amazing 40,000 tons of this first anufactured semi-synthetic plastic. ("Semi" in that it does contain an ganic ingredient.)

It is sometimes called "Ivorine," "Old Ivory," as well as "French Ivory" d early plastic.

This material which is in the category of a thermoplastic, is very light d can be produced in varying thickness to very thin. Manufacturing tech- ques included being made into sheets from which it could be carved, wed, turned, planed, and stamped. Another production technique was jection molding. The chemicals were mixed, heated, and then injected th pressure (steam, I believe) into molds. After quite a long period of oling the items were "hard" (no longer in a plastic state). They could then easily buffed and polished. The surface remains so soft that it can be ffed with a nylon stocking — the same as candle wax.

Because it is so soft, it dents and scratches easily as well as stains and lits. Sunlight fades it, and it is highly flammable.

My collection is primarily of the creamy ivory color, although I have a w pieces of pink, green, and yellow.

Various trade names appear on objects which I have collected, although -ra-lin (with or without hyphens) is the most common. I also have a piece

marked "Tuskaloid" and several with the mark "Du Barry" usually with t
word "Pyralin." I would guess that these items were the actual container fo
Du Barry product, such as face powder. Apparently the item was so inexpe
sive to make that it was given away as a container for the product, in the pro
uct itself, or attached to a product (such as a stamp holder in or on a spice ca
or as an advertisement for a product or company in some useful form —
object that would be used repeatedly. Often these are objects that would r
be in common use today, but were a necessity in the daily life of that time.

Some examples I have in my collection are a whetstone to sharpen a sm
knife, a matchbox cover, a cover for a tummyache remedy that not only ider
fied the medication but brought a smile to the face of the user (which probal
helped the tummyache the most!).

My search goes on for even more intriguing items: brushes especially
brushing specific things — mustaches, babies' hair, beaver hats. I have a kn
for trimming one's "corn," a razor with a special blade for trimming sidebur
score keepers for various games, soap boxes, containers for tooth powder
hand mirror with self-cover.

Garage sales signs and collectible shows draw me like a magnet. I set up
pattern of going from table to table in one direction only and try to do a qu
once over. If I see something that attracts my attention I check the price a
condition and note where it is in the surroundings so I can return if I do not s
something that will have more value in my collection — something rea
unique and something that I do not have. I strive to not buy duplicates a
prefer the creamy ivory color with obvious striations.

When I see a flash of ivory, I mosey over toward it. With a deft tap of r
fingernail I eliminate pottery and metal. It may take a closer observation
determine if this is a later manufacturer's plastic, real ivory, or my hea
desire. Plastic does not have the striations. Ivory has greater weight — a
price. Sometimes other materials are used in conjunction with the Fren
Ivory such as bone and of course, metals for the blades, shafts, and findings.

Sometimes it is not obvious that an item is made of celluloid. I was gra
ful when a dealer pointed out to me that a picture was actually made of cel
loid. You will see the item with a very nice verse "To Mother" on page 1
One can always learn more!

Some dealers do not even attempt to clean this material believing, I thir
that if it is totally dirty it might appear that all of the blemishes will wash aw
with a little soap and water. Actually, I would prefer to clean the item mys
rather than have a dealer use sandpaper — much too harsh — or soak in h
water (which may distort the shape) — or use harsh chemicals. If they do
may never even get the chance to see the item. I'm sure that many items a
thrown away as not having any value or no more than a cottage cheese carton

I use alcohol on a cottonball or piece of paper towel to remove the stic
residue made by price labels, rinsing as I go, in case I run into an especially d
ficult spot that takes a lot of time to get off. I rub hard but parallel with the s

ce while supporting it from behind so I will not dent the piece.

Speaking of those horrible price labels: always determine that they have
ot been place in such a way that they are covering a permanent stain. *And I do
ean permanent.* If a sticker is the only way to attach a price, the best place
ould be inside or on the bottom, not covering the "mark." I have seen some
idence recently that some dealers are using something to lighten stains,
owever this also takes away the gloss and the shape of the stain remains on
e surface visible from various angles.

This is a material that is 50 to 100 years old! Do you expect it to be pris-
ne and without character? If it is a holder for a perfume bottle, isn't there a
ood chance that it will have gotten a drop of perfume on it in all those years?
erfume seems to get the blame for the major spots. Actually most of my per-
ume holders are in better condition than dresser trays. These actually seem to
ave gotten the most spots — next to the back of mirrors.

And then there is "Here a spot, there a spot, everywhere a spot - spot." I
ake every effort to closely examine what I wish to buy, but I have taken
eces home and after I have carefully washed them I find that there are spat-
rs of paint all over! It is as if the paint has been released and is coming out of
e depths of the material and reforming on the surface!

The positive aspect of this is that in most cases these spots can easily be
emoved from a clean piece by gently pushing with a fingernail. The fleck of
aint will shear away in one piece leaving the surface clean. However, if the
ntire piece has been painted, this method does not work. Believe me, I have
ad experience in this matter! (See page 33.)

Care of Celluloid

Dealers, in general, do not care much about acquiring celluloid. It
is not, as in the current phrasing: "dealer friendly." It can easily
become totally worthless and ruined in the routine cleaning
rocess. It might react to some cleaning agents and melt. It is easily crushed in
acking. If packed with anything containing camphor it may begin to disinte-
rate. Even hot water can release camphor and cause it to warp out of shape. If
begins to crack — it will continue to crack until it breaks apart.

This is what I recommend: wash gently in warm or lukewarm water with a
ttle pine solvent. Rub with your finger or a soft wet paper towel. Ease into
e cracks and crevices and dry just as gently. Do not immerse items that have
ollow spaces or lithographed photos. If there are stickers on an item — buyer
eware (see the bottom of page 16). The sticker may cover a severe blemish or
not, the rest of the piece may have sunfaded and under the spot will be a dif-
erent color.

It is theoretically possible that all but the unfaded spot might be covered so t spot could "catch up" in the sun somewhat like applying sunblock to an overe posed area of skin while exposing the rest of the body — and probably about successful!

Alcohol can help remove the "sticky" after a paper sticker is soaked and much as possible, is gently peeled off. Apply rubbing alcohol, rub the stickine into a ball, rubbing the sticky ball about, letting it help pick itself up (like ma ing a miniature snow ball!). Then quickly rinse as the alcohol will remove th gloss of the finish.

I have found that the easiest spot to remove is a fleck of paint. Gentle pre sure from a natural fingernail can slightly depress the Pyralin and the paint sp will flex off, especially if the item has been washed first and the edges are free any grease or oil tending to hold them in place. As previously mentioned, th method is not recommended for items which are intentionally painted.

Owners of Pyralin seem to have been very creative in making any pie their very own and adapting it to their own special uses.

I have heard that little boys were very fond of appropriating a piece or two Great-aunt's set for the excitement of seeing it "whoosh" into flames. It wa after all, made up of cellulose nitrate with camphor and alcohol. For those of yo who like me, may not have your degree in chemistry, cellulose nitrate is also basic ingredient of gun powder.

I must share a personal experience with you. I packed away a box of cell loid pieces with some small items purchased in Japan and an item made epoxy. When I opened the box again I first noticed a dewy look on some of th items and a faint smell of camphor (similar to moth ball smell). When I touche these items the "dew" was distinctly sticky and although I immediately washe them in water and alcohol the reaction did not stop. There were large areas th were transparent looking with the irregular patches of cellulose easily seen. was obvious that the item was slowly disintegrating. I have been told that th Japanese statues made of a substance also containing camphor caused the cam phor in the celluloid to disassociate and began the reaction. According to chemist, the only treatment: increase air flow around the item. (Note photos c pages 13 and 14.)

Items which survived many years may have survived because they we setting out in the open air probably on a crocheted doily, cushioning them fro direct contact with any other chemicals, including any finish on furniture and n boxed away for a distant future.

A powder polish was part of the ongoing routine care of a dresser set.

At last I have found a very simple solution to stopping the disintegratic process: soak in a solution of baking soda and water. The loose cotton flockir floats free and after a thorough drying by towel and in the sun, the disassociatic of the chemical is stopped. It would probably be a very good procedure to rou tinely wash in baking soda and use the baking soda as a mild abrasive on an spots.

According to the *Merit Student's Encyclopedia*, Macmillan Education Co., copyright N.Y. 1990: "Since prehistoric times ivory has been carved and modeled into decorative and useful objects: billiard balls, piano keys, chess sets, buttons."

Ivory is classified as hard or soft. Hard ivory is brittle and difficult to cut. It is obtained mostly from Asian elephants. Soft ivory which has been obtained chiefly from African elephants, is easier to cut. It does not readily crack and can withstand temperature changes better. The largest known elephant tusks are 10 feet long and weigh 225 pounds. That's a lot of carving material!

All ivory comes from the teeth of mammals. There are three layers to these teeth (been to your dentist lately? He will tell you the same thing): Outer layer is of hard enamel, middle layer is of softer material called dentin, inner layer of nerves and blood vessels that feed the tooth.

Ivory is not a solid material — it contains a series of very small tubes filled with a waxlike liquid. This structure makes ivory fairly easy to carve. It also gives polished ivory the warm glowing tone for which it is so prized. Have you seen ivory that has aged into beautiful varied golden tones of browns?

Because the hard outer layer of enamel of elephant's tusks is worn away by digging roots, moving fallen trees, and fighting, the elephant tusk was an especially desirable source of ivory. The carver did not have to remove this outer layer as it was already worn away.

Walrus is the second most common source of ivory and averages 3' in length and approximately 5 pounds in weight.

The whale tooth, though rarer and smaller in size, is used for scrimshaw. Designs are carved by making grooves in the whale tooth and ink (usually black) is put into the grooves.

The single tooth of the narwhal has interesting folklore. It was thought that it was the horn of the mythical unicorn and was thought to have special properties to detect poison. Items were carved so it might be used in this way for protection.

Because of the size of the elephant's tusk and because the outer hard layer might have been worn away, it was the most desirable source of material for the carver. Otherwise before any carving could begin, the outer layer had to be removed.

And so to obtain this desirable material, elephants were killed. In an effort to reduce the illegal killing of elephants the African elephant was classified as an endangered species by the Convention on International Trade in Endangered Species. This action put into effect a ban on all trade in ivory. This action was taken in 1989. By then, the population of the African elephant had been deparately reduced by poaching to less than half.

Even in the 1800s there was a desire to find an acceptible imitation for elephant tusk ivory. That is where our story started!

After all - we had to have those billiard balls! And that was the beginning of celluloid!

Prices

Some dealers may believe that my prices are too low, but I still fi
pieces made of this material every place I look throughout the Unit
States: collectible shops, garage sales, shows, in antique shops, and
foreign countries.

In dealer malls the prices are lower than in individual shops indicati
the buyer benefits from the competition.

In my opinion items made of celluloid, French Ivory, and other bra
names will continue to be released onto the market for several more years
individuals breakup their households and consolidate into smaller livi
quarters and after that would-be collections will be returning items to t
market as they move on to other interests.

To state higher prices would be false and serve only a dealer who ha
large amount of this material on hand at this time.

I have found that competition has lowered prices in the last few yea
not raised them.

It is true that some items are rare and I suspect only relatively few we
manufactured. Some are especially fragile and may not have survived ov
the years. These can only become more valuable to those of us who wish
collect them.

The sturdy ones have survived and are surfacing although sometimes
very poor condition. As in the law of survival of the fittest, there will be
natural weeding out process that will leave the best and strongest and mo
unique.

With this celluloid material there is no need to worry about having
eliminate reproductions made in the old molds.

Damage to Celluloid

Care of celluloid can become a dealer's nightmare as this material is not easy to keep in top shape. It can be crushed, scratches easily, and does not tolerate high temperatures. It can react to other substances which may cause it to disintegrate. Once this reaction begins even washing in alcohol may not stop the disintegration as the molecules actually begin to decompose and return to a powdery state, but in the meantime the surface is sticky to the touch, which certainly does not make compatible with other collectibles!

The photos that follow show examples of pieces disassociating or actually attempting to return to separate into the original chemicals.

The two smaller pieces may have lovely matching painted decorations, but they continue to be sticky so must be kept out of contact with everything else. I have been advised that with good ventilation the disassociating process may stop and their disintegration might become stablized.

Note the transparent appearance. Segregate these pieces from all others as this process is contagious. Even though the pieces are not in phyical contact, the fumes from the piece which is disintegrating may begin the disassociating process in another piece within a confined area, such as a packing box.

The cellulose is very prominent. It looks as though the tiny pieces of lint or cellulose could be picked out. The entire piece is very soft and fragile. A portion of the edge has broken off. This piece looks as though it could easily crumble into nothingness.

Moisture in itself will not harm the celluloid but where a thin transparent celluloid is applied over a porous surface, such as paper, the underlying paper will no doubt discolor. In the example of a book cover where a thin layer of celluloid is applied over a printed paper (often called a lithograph) a sprinkle of rain may devalue an item from $24.00 to $6.00. The rain on the book pages cause the pages to wrinkle and adhere to each other. Moisture will cause wires in hinges and linings in vases to rust!

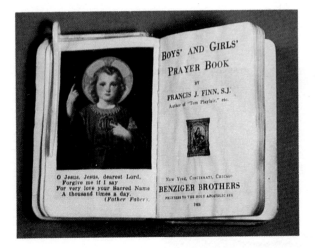

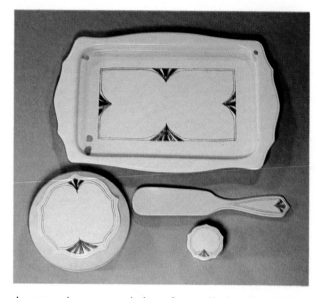

An attractive set consisting of a small glass-lined rouge container, shoehorn, powder box, and tray, all with a simple black fan design. All the pieces are in good condition except the tray which has several dark discolored spots. Each item was priced $5.00 to $5.50.

Note the discoloration at the edge of the price tag: "buyer beware."

ease note the warp of the
des of the red velvet-
ned boxes.

When I purchased the blue
velvet-lined box it was
warped as badly as the red
lined boxes.

I wedged wooden sticks into the box and left it closed on a sunny win-
ow sill to gradually restore this piece to square. (I would move the sticks
ound a bit to even up the squaring process every month or two.)

Boxes are often displayed open. I would advise keeping them closed
hen left for long periods of time to prevent warping.

I do not advise trying to speed up the warp-correction process. In boxes,
e velvet linings would get wet if immersed in water and the glue that
olds the linings in place would come loose . I personally wouldn't try float-
g them in hot water either. The hinges could get water inside and rust the
ttle wire which holds the hinge in place and then it might break. When a
inge breaks, even if only in one place, the other half is subject to extra
rain and with even minimal handling the other half will surely not hold for
ng.

Would you wish to try hot air? I'm not that adventurous and am content
ith the slow and easy solar method.

Note the split in the corner of this large beautiful celluloid covered box. There does not appear to be any support material under the raised area or repoussé work.

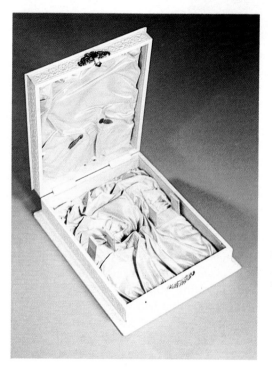

The inside of this 9½" x 11" x 3½" box is lined with pale blue satin. Holders for specific items are under the satin. This box was built to hold a mirror in the lid. Note the two metal pieces to lock it in place. I can only guess that the bottom half was meant to hold a hair brush and comb and a couple of other specific items. It was purchased empty.

Buffer (polisher) construction and repair materials. Note the very worn buffers. The buffer in the center is not only worn but badly warped into a concave shape. On the right, a piece of chamois skin and a metal ring. These are the basic repair parts. Many of my buffers show signs of having had the chamois replaced as they have tips of leather sticking out.

A block of wood is covered with a chamois skin that is fastened tightly to the oval-shaped block with a cord. Sometimes there is additional padding over the block of wood similar to felt, and a double layer of chamois skin. In addition to the tightly fastened cord there is often a metal or celluloid ring which is more decorative than functional as it does not actually hold the chamois in place.

This buffer of chamois skin is rubbed across the fingernails to smooth and shine the nails. Often there is a small handle on the top to assist in performing this relaxing repetitive movement. After frequent sessions of buffing, the fingernails shine even without the use of any polishing compound. Often the small round boxes in the dresser set contain a powder which I believe was used sparingly on the fingernail to assist with adding gloss to the nail.

Note the split on the end of the buffer tray. This split will continue! It would be my preference to stop the splitting with a little super glue. Certainly a dealer might indicate that this has been done to prevent further damage from occurring. If it were only given an "as is" tag, chances are that it would soon be in two pieces with the trash can the next inevitable destination.

19

Note the appearance of the handle on this brush. See the erratic lines? They are more or less parallel — more like dashes than the ongoing striations of French Ivory. This is an organic substance, such as bone or perhaps ivory. It does have a stamped imprint: MAUREY-DESCHAMPS and underneath "Paris France." A nice little hairbrush, but not celluloid.

This six-leaf bo[ok] labeled Monday throu[gh] Saturday is a fam[ous] piece made of ivor[y]. The barely legible wr[it]ing on the pages refer[s] April of 1881 or 1887.

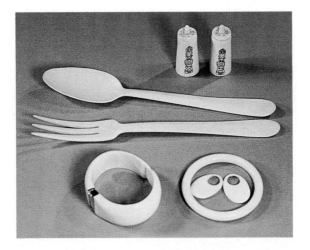

Pieces of ivory, most from Alaska as you might guess by the painted totem poles on the salt and pepper shakers, purchased by that maiden auntie in the '30s. May I bore you with a family story? Auntie's father accompanied Nan and her friend by boat to Alaska. Consistent with her profession as bookkeeper, expectations were precise, especially when it came to time of departure. What a surprise then to arrive at the dock to find that the ship had departed one hour earlier when the tide was high instead of exactly the published time and that it would be a week before the next ship departed Anchorage again. This trip was to be one of the high points of Nan's long life and one which I always enjoyed and felt privileged to hear in her later years.

The wide bracelet with hinge and keyhole earrings were also purchased in Alaska, but at J.C. Penney in 1981. There are circles where the curvature of the bracelet passes through a striation or growth ring, if you will. French Ivory only goes so far in imitating nature: there are varying widths of striations but never circles even though there is a curvature.

The salad set shows the more relaxed graining of real ivory. At a mall collectible show, I purchased the bangle or circle bracelet for $1.00. It had a very chalky dull finish and I thought it had the possibility of being celluloid, but the more I wore it, the shinier it became and the more the graining or striations became visible until I finally knew positively that I really had a bargain for my $1.00.

This has been a special piece in my collection for many years, but upon closer examination it was necessary to move it into this section of the book. It is wonderful brush for cleaning fingers. I believe it to have been designed for that purpose rather than for cleaning false teeth, for example. The handle is attached with a piece of metal down each shaft to form the handle, inconsistent with assembly of pieces made of celluloid which are easily attached to each other by either heat or an epoxy-like substance. The piece exhibits all the characteristics of natural ivory.

Though the lids of these two square boxes are ivory in color, they are very thin, rigid, and brittle. The sides are clear and rippled — an obvious give-away that this is not celluloid, but plain plastic.

According to the *Academic American Encyclopedia* (1993) celluloid was the first successful plastic, inception date 1868. "Similar composition was developed in 1850 by Alexander Parkes but it lacked durability. Self-trained chemist John W. Hyatt combined nitrocellulose, camphor, and alcohol to form a mixture that he molded under heat in a hydraulic press." According to this source: "Its principle use was 20 years later in photographic film invented by George Eastman." I'm certainly glad that the Celluloid Mfg. Co. which John W. registered with his brother Isaiah Smith Hyatt, did produce a few items in the meantime! In fact, a reported 40,000 tons!

Trademarks

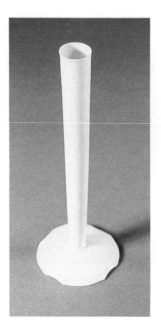

"Amber Pyralin (Pyralin in script) Du Barry." That's what it says, but it doesn't look amber to me! The item itself is creamy ivory.

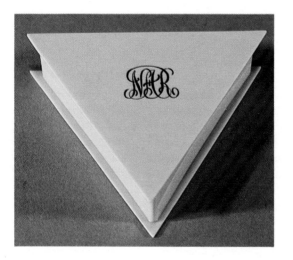

Triangular-shaped box. "French (K in circle)*Ivory" Dark Blue Scroll Initials: NA

Small round box with crocheted cover on lid.
Three half sphere legs with bead; "FRENCH IVORY."

Unusual shape — double walled construction
Oval encircling "IVORY LA-BELLE Py-ra-lin."

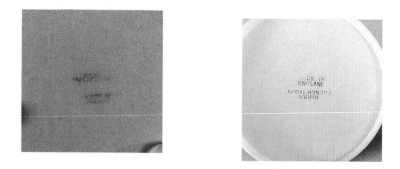

Round, three glued-on sphere legs. Vase with same mark "BIRK FRENCH IVORY" separate stamp "Made in England" (upside down on vase). The powder box and vase right side up (below).

"IVORY" in small capital letters
"Pyralin" in script so ornate that
dealers often mistake the "P" for an
"L" although I do not believe there
is a mark Lyralin. The third and bottom line says: "DUBARRY."

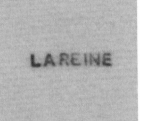

"LA REINE"

Small oval box with mark in oval "Ivory DU BARRY Py-ra-lin."

he blue velvet-lined jewelry box with
ur shaped applied legs shown on page
and the powder box on page 90 both
ve this unusual mark "ACWALITE"
ith the letters taller on each end).

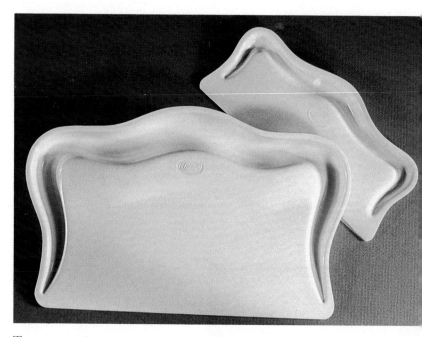

Two-pc. crumber set used to remove crumbs from the table cloth. Deeply press "Fuller" in oval.

Two genuine "Fuller" brushes.

Additional trademarks not shown.
"Mayflower"
"French (K inside fish with arrow nose) IVORY"
"Ivory FIBEROID"
"Ivorene"
"Colonial Quality"
"Camille" outlined with an oval.

Decorations

Was the general populace more creative in the 1920s? I'm suspicious that they were and were inclined to personalize their belongings with decorations from decals to paint dribbles. Note the item on the top of page 33 that was painted the sickly peach color. I thought I could remove this paint by carefully chipping it off as I didn't wish to risk dissolving the piece in solvent; however this removal process is still in progress and I show this piece as a good example of a creative ancestor.

Can you imagine life without the many plastics in our lives? I am amazed to find items that appear to be made of the same material marked as made in other countries. I have items from Germany and France and England. One is a lovely salmon colored cosmetic set for a child on the bottom of page 51.

Can you imagine the day to day life one hundred years ago? At least in the western half of the United States life was a day to day struggle for sustenance and personal survival. Everyone in the family attempted to make a contribution to the welfare of the whole family. The simple pleasures were treasured and planned with great anticipation. The beauty of the surroundings were enhanced by whatever skills were available to each involved.

What a gift an item of celluloid must have been, the lightweight translucent piece of celluloid with a surface luster to rival fine Belleek from Copermanach, Ireland. Though both are fragile in many ways, the celluloid is not as subject to shattering when dropped which no doubt made it much more durable during a move westward, for example.

Items are personalized with dribbles of pastel paint in patterns suggestive of flowers or bows. The designs are simple and straight forward and I would guess applied by the owner although possibly prior to sale. Some of my items have decals applied (see page 32). I am suspicious that these decals might have been applied by the owner since the items have assorted trademarks. I was so excited to purchase this group, I didn't even ask if the price was firm or if the seller would take a lower price! And then after examining every piece, I carefully boxed them away to be taken out at a later time to marvel again at the variety of shapes and construction.

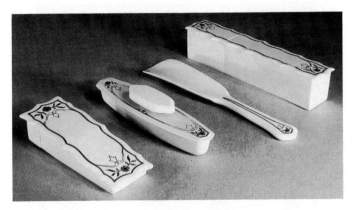

A four-piece set with matching nostalgic violets and black line design. What an interesting combination of pieces. Note the wedge-shaped piece to hold what? A tube of something? Set $25.00.

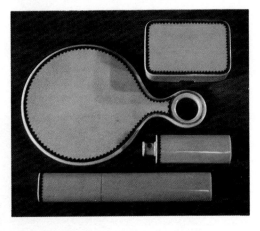

ple yet elegant black sawtooth ign with outline of gold. This consists of hand mirror, soap , telescoping toothbrush hold- and tooth powder container. $25.00.

Fingernail set outlined in black. Includes buffer and buffer powder holder. Set $12.00.

A complete set with pansy decals. What more could you wish? Set $145.00 – 250.00.

Some of the pieces with inside detail. The entire set has more value together than each piece individually, although many are unique. Set $145.00 – 250.00.

Box painted pale peach with floral decals applied strategically. The inside is divided into three sections and lined with dark blue velvet; both top and bottom are lined. $25.00.

Initialed in that wonderful Victorian scroll, so ornate and intertwined that it is often a puzzle to decipher what the letters are! Set $40.00 - 45.00.

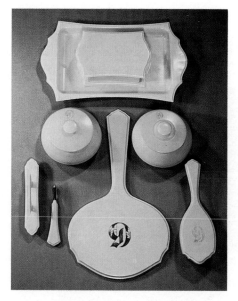

I can never resist purchasing pie with a "D" since that is the init of my last name. While attend the Zonta International Convent held in Detroit in 1994, I walk across the street from the Rena sance Convention Center a placed a silent bid for a 12-pc. to be offered at the auction DuMouchelle's. The 12-pie count includes each piece, r item; the round boxes and lids counted individually, as are t buffer and buffer tray. What a s prise to learn that I had won t bid — now all I had to do was the items from Detroit to Olymp WA. Set $65.00 – 80.00.

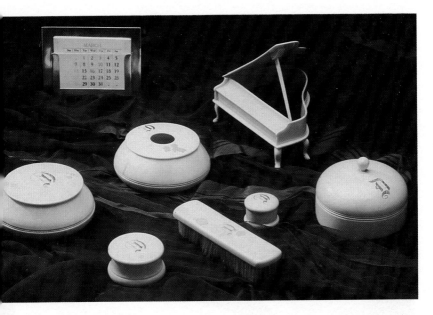

t also initialed with matching "D" though pieces were acquired individually. The
rpetual calendar is contained in a sterling silver frame. The D is in the upper
ht-hand corner. Many of the months and dates are very worn, but I still enjoy
ing it. (It is much more convenient than holding an old calendar until it is good
ain.) $32.00 – 45.00.

1e powder box and hair receiver are round with pear-shaped bottom section.
2.00 – 15.00.

1e grand piano also has the initial "D" on the lid. I purchased it at a collectible
ow in Victoria, B.C. I had gone as a passenger with a friend and returned from the
ow with the question: Do you have room in your car to take home a "grand
ano?" $35.00 – 50.00.

1e two smaller boxes have a curved base. $10.00 each.

1e rectangular brush (and the hair receiver) have quite bad stains. $6.00 – 8.00.

1e box on the far right is round but with straight-sided bottom half. $8.00 – 10.00.

I have scroll initial "D." Check the variations of the initial "D" on pages 34 and
. The box with the straight sides above varies the greatest from all of the others.

Another view of the baby grand piano-shaped jewelry box. $35.00 – 50.00.

The One(s) That Got Away

I continue to regret not having in my collection a letter opener shaped like a lovely lady in a long full skirt. She had a stonecut marquisette set at her throat as a necklace. I felt that the $25.00 being asked was beyond my budget, but I have spent more than that wearing out shoe leather looking for her again.

Another purchase I failed to make was a set of placecards. With their intricate cutwork, they looked very fragile and delicate, and I believe the dealer decided not to exhibit them again and I'll always wish I had them in my collection. I have a jewelry item with similar cutwork mounted in a gold bezel as a pin bottom of page 106. It really needs to have beveled glass added to protect it.

Another item I was unable to purchase was an eyepiece for examining jewelry known as a "loupe." It was in use in a jewelry store in Victoria, B.C., and was not for sale. I would have treasured this item, as I have treasured items that were "Mother's" or "Auntie's." If someone doesn't treasure an item "for sentimental value," I assure you that I will. I have my neighbor's mother's pin cushion complete with pins and needles. Another friend brought me a small box with glass lining and later when I learned of her untimely death it became a cherished reminder of her. Another young lady, gave me a small hand mirror that was not only of this material, but had flowers in bas relief on the back making it unique in my collection.

I have always tried to enjoy the pieces I acquire and treat them with loving care. I was surprised that exhibiting them (or perhaps just packing and transporting them) resulted in some damage and it was necessary to make some repairs. In my opinion it is better to use a little super glue and prevent further damage rather than to maintain the flaw as is which will result in a crack expanding until perhaps the item is totally destroyed. When carefully applied, a drop of super glue will stop further tearing and deterioration of the item. Since these items are for my own pleasure and not for sale this is not done to deceive. One must always remember that you are dealing with essentially plastic that may melt if touched by acetone, for example. For years I thought it was entirely safe to use denatured alcohol as a cleaner, but even alcohol will dull the finish or high gloss of the French Ivory if allowed to stand on it. It is a simple matter to rinse the item and stop any reaction.

ADVERTISING ITEMS

Since celluloid was so inexpensive to produce and so versatile it was well suited for give-away advertising, commemorative, and souvenir items. Even the advertising items remaining after nearly 100 years vary immensely. Thin flat sheets of celluloid were made into bookmarks. The amount of information printed on them gave not only the name and address of the advertiser and the service provided but perhaps a calendar or perpetual calendar, information worthy of saving such as birth gemstones, and perhaps a homily or bit of humor. Thicker pieces were cut and sawed into shapes for letter openers. Edges were turned up to form trays.

A commemorative from Kiwanis International on the occasion of Charter Presentation (when a new club is given its charter). This matchbox holder was for a club in Mankato, Minnesota with charter dated April 27, 1921. The holder is metal with a metal edge around the celluloid. I purchased this in Toronto, Ontario, Canada, in 1982. $15.00 – 35.00.

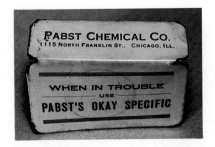

Another matchbox holder or perhaps a pillbox holder since it is advertising a patent medicine of the time: PABST'S OKAY SPECIFIC from Pabst Chemical Co., 1115 North Franklin St., Chicago, Illinois When turned end for end the pained "before" expression on the printed face becomes a smiling "After Pabst's Okay" face. $18.00 – 25.00.

Again this is a celluloid wrap over a metal holder, but in this item the celluloid has not survived the wear very well. (This same clever before and after design is also used on other items of the time.)

A pocket mirror also with brilliantly printed "gemstones" for each month, adve tising for A. Diamant DIAMOND BROKER 824 Main St., Kansas City, Mis souri. $18.00 – 20.00.

J. H. Stream, dealer in fine liquors and cigars, had a match safe created as a hol day gift for its customers. The lid was hinged at the top end. The metal inden tion on the lid is ribbed so it might be used as a scratcher to light the matche which are safely contained within this metal case. A celluloid wrap was used a the printing surface and shows the years of service and wear with its chipped co ners. Although this item is well used, it does not show any burn marks or disco oration so it was used with care and kept away from flame and moisture. $28.00.

A pocket mirror/paperweight with advertising for Mount Vernon Daily Heral Although this specific item has a very dark mirror it had a hefty price. It has loc appeal. $25.00.

A stamp holder — Compliments of Schilling's Best. One side shows the head of a horse which may have been famous at the time with the quote "At your service." Do you suppose this was "Man of War"? $12.00 – 15.00.

A small comb and envelope-type comb holder with printing on both sides. $7.50.

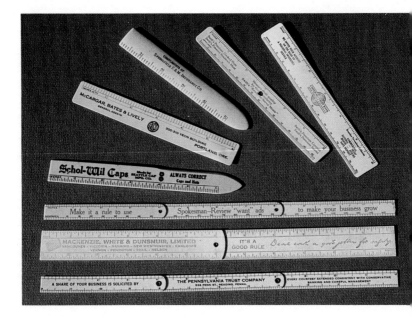

Assorted measuring rulers with advertising for various establishments. $5.00 – 12.00 each. Folding rules $15.00 – 18.00.

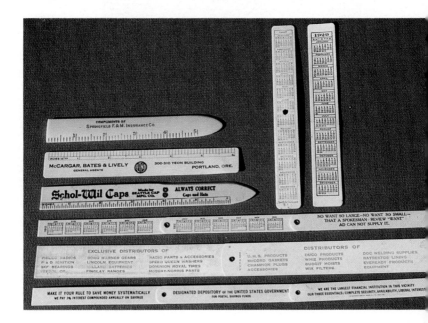

Although this small bound book was designed to be used for shopping lists, instead the owner chose to write notes. One especially poignant comment from 1949 on April 13th "Earthquake struck Centralia just before noon, was severe. I was unnerved." What an understatement! $8.00 – 10.00.

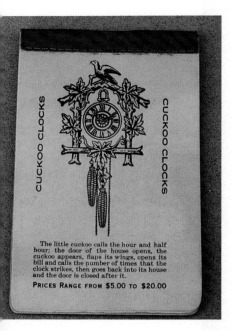

The back of the booklet advertises a delightful ornately carved wooden cuckoo clock and what a good price!

BABY ITEMS

Ordinary day-to-day necessary items were made especially for baby. There is the blanket holder. The one shown is made of a sheet of thick celluloid cut and then shaped into a springy elongated oval. One side is simply shaped and painted with a little Dutch boy. It would hold a blanket in place in the crib or carriage to keep the drafts off baby.

Many of the child-size items in my collection have painted decorations of pale blue and pink and all with simple renditions of floral or ribbon designs. I am showing fine-toothed combs and soft-bristled brushes. There are powder boxes and soap boxes. There is a bank with matching flowers. The bank has two holes on each side so a ribbon could tie the top to the base to securely save the contents for "Baby." Amusingly, although I have never had a piece with a "loose bottom," the bottom of this bank can easily be tipped in and contents, if any, easily removed without disturbing and untying the ribbons.

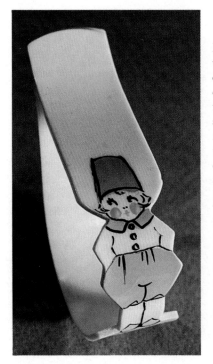

Blanket holder. $18.00 – 20.00. Note that this is made of a flat piece of celluloid, roughly shaped and painted with a Dutch boy design, bent to form a loose loop. How simple yet attractive! The flexibility of this material allows this simple construction to be springy enough to hold covers loosely in place. In the 40s there was another type of blanket holder made in the shape of a duck. The bill of the duck was designed to hold the blanket with a rough surface of teeth. The bill opened to insert the blanket, pivoting from a rivet. The duck was tied to the bed or crib with a ribbon. It was quite elaborate in design and made of plastic, not celluloid.

Brush and comb with matching pink and blue painted flowers, dots, and lines. $10.00 – 12.00.

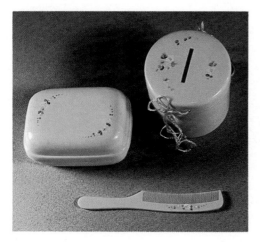

Soap box. $6.00 – 8.00.
Bank. $12.00 – 15.00.
Curved-handled comb.
$1.00 – 3.00.

Baby brush and double fine-
toothed comb with pink
painted decoration. $8.00 –
12.00. Pink mirror with
raised design on celluloid.
$5.00 – 7.00.

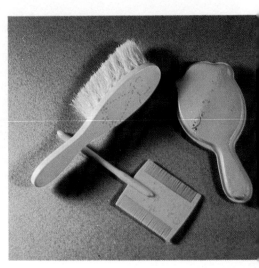

Toy mirror with ribbon
and miniature ribbed
tray. $45.00.

DOLLS AND TOYS

The celluloid doll, circa 1869 was originally an English invention, but it was left to two Americans, John Wesley Hyatt and his brother Isaiah Smith Hyatt to manufacture celluloid dolls mmercially. They were made of a synthetic material composed of cellu- e nitrate, camphor, pigment, fillers, and alcohol (with) hot steam, blown o the molds. Since they were inexpensive they were collected in large mbers...one of the most popular being the Kewpie range as stated in *cyclopedia of Victoriana*, Macmillan Publishing Co., Inc. NY, 1975.

In *More Twentieth Century Dolls - from Bisque to Vinyl* by Johana Gast derton, celluloid appears in Volume one A-H. With pictures and text, one ntroduced to dolls of many sizes and shapes. The text begins: "As with que, the small imported celluloid dolls of the 1920s were available until supply which had been in stock prior to the outbreak of World War II depleted. Since distributors such as Butler Brothers often ordered dolls I toys from Europe and Japan by the shipload, ample stock may have en in the warehouses to carry through the first few years of conflict."

Again in order to aid collectors in the identification of these small dolls, eems well to show a large assortment. Those shown were being listed in catalogs of 1926 through 1929. "The larger dolls shown present ample dence of the fact that celluloid makes beautiful dolls; no other material es quite the same effect. In addition, the variety seems virtually end- s."

Reading this book and looking at the pictures was almost as good as being doll museum! And as I recall that situation, the greatest problem the curator was keeping the visitors from picking up and hugging the duplicate of one's n baby doll displayed within arm's reach and far too much of a temptation for ny.

Even when presented in the one dimension of the printed page, still some iliar expression may come through. I recall from long ago the tiny celluloid th showing inside a slightly open mouth and eyes that moved a bit when the lids opened and closed. (Never mind that the original hair that had been rcombed and replaced with shiny black paint.)

Both boy and girl baby dolls, from small blown-mold dolls and toys are strated in Anderton's books. Some have jointed arms or arms and legs, ally attached with elastic thread. Others have a fixed posture with paint- on features and costumes. Often dyed feathers and chenille were glued The dolls vary from Orphan Annie, Uncle Sam, Santa Claus, bellhops, eball and football players to babies in birthday suits to adult costumes of orted occupations. Hats, ribbons, even elaborately styled marcel waves re all molded and painted. Prices ranged from .35 and .36 per dozen for " dolls to $2 per dozen for the "25¢ celluloid 8½" doll assortment." Some s came with their own furniture or toy made of paper or enameled metal.

A 2½" doll, fully jointed came in a small hinged plaid box with white ena
eled metal bath tub, rubber sponge, and wash cloth — cost to wholesaler
cents per dozen. There were celluloid dolls with a musical chime insi
(The small paper and wood folding parasols included with the bathing c
tume doll look exactly like the ones we currently see as party decorations

The author Johana Gast Anderton does a wonderful job of leading c
down memory lane so if there is anything you wish to know about dolls,
check your library for her books.

Dolls:
Painted celluloid. $6.00 – 8.00.
Flesh-tone with moveable arms and legs. $15.00 – 18.00.
Doll "rattle" with two celluloid loops attached. $18.00 – 23.00.

Celluloid-head finger puppet in felt robe.
$25.00 – 28.00.

Inside of puppet.

I wonder how many hollow celluloid toys have survived 100 years. Some celluloid figures were filled with plaster-of-Paris or chalk. This would help stabilize from crushing; otherwise their fragility was similar to that of a ping-pong ball.

This fragility and scarcity of the toy increases the price to the collector, unfortunately.

Roly-Poly, baby face, one side sad, reverse happy. $100.00 – 150.00.

Knowing something about the original owner of a piece always adds the pleasure of having a piece in one's collection! This is the dealer's sto about the roly-poly: I was touring the northeast and came across a sale in private home. The lady was consolidating her living surroundings to mo into a smaller space and had a lifetime of treasures. After I had purchase the ordinary things — glassware, small furniture, etc., I asked about a bo labeled "Christmas ornaments" and suggested that perhaps some of th family would treasure these, however would she mind if I looked through case there was something else besides Christmas tree ornaments inside That is where I found the roly-poly carefully wrapped in tissue. It had a b of curling ribbon around its neck and had obviously been hung on the tre by this family.

The dealer was fond of this item and I could tell she was disappointed part with it even for $85; however, I value this as a once-in-a-lifetime treasure

The base is rounded and weighted so the slightest touch sets it wo bling, the same as its larger counterparts. One side has permanent tears. this was designed to placate a crying child what do you guess the reactio would be when the other side tips into view? Somehow I suspect an eve louder wail might occur when that smiling face is seen! In spite of a attempt at chubby cheeks and dimples, this face is a little bit scary! Th baby cap, though just pressed on as a part of the features, has a tiny bit c crochet on each side as if it is an attached cap. All in all, it is an exceptiona ly unique item and being hollow celluloid is especially vulnerable to crusl ing. I would place its value in the $100.00 to $125.00 range or leave it a NFS.

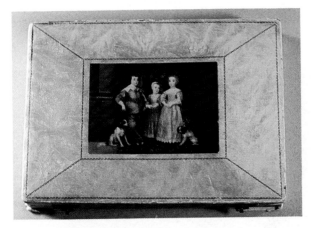

Child's dresser set made in Germany. $45.00 – 60.00.
Cardboard box holds mirrored-lid, salmon pink miniature set
containing three fingernail tools, nail polisher (buffer), rouge,
and pomade containers.

BOOKS

German Bible, in excellent like-new condition. It was purchased in a brown cardboard box with velvet inside bottom half. $35.00 – 50.00.

Prayer Book, "A manual of prayers and instructions" showing much more use. $25.00 – 35.00.

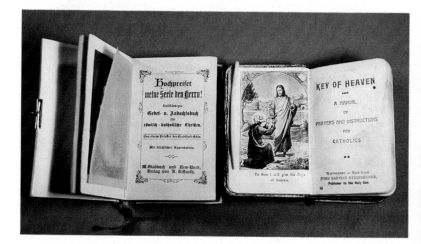

Tiny Book card. Note the repoussé on the cover and around the edge of back page of card; the cover not only has painted leaves and flowers, but says "Happy Days." Made in Germany. $12.00 – 15.00.

To greet
My Love.

Pray think of me
when flowers you view:
Their beauties
all expressed in you:
Pray think of me
when you are sad;
With you I could
not but be glad.

Made in Germany

BOOKMARKS

Plate 57. Heart-shaped with forget-me-nots and a Bible verse, 1 John 3:1:

"Behold what manner of love the Father hath bestowed on us that we should be called Sons of God" and "When he shall appear we shall be like him." $4.00 – 6.00.

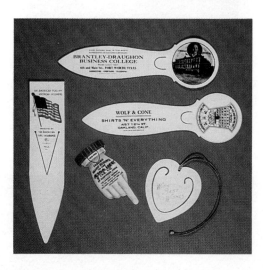

1. A patriotic bookmark. $10.00 – 12.00.

2 & 3. Two identically shaped bookmarks with perpetual calendars. $35.00 – 50.00 each.

4. Small hand-shaped bookmark with name of advertiser on a lifelike hand with the subliminal suggestion of professionalism with tip of the requisite pinstripe suit and white cuff. $12.00 – 15.00.

5. "Best Wishes" on reverse side of heart-shaped bookmark, pictured above. Letters show wear. If in better condition, $10.00 – 12.00.

BOXES

An assortment of boxes of varying sizes and shapes. $10.00 – 45.00 each.

Box with attached shaped legs, closed and open, revealing a velvet-lining inside. $25.00 – 30.00.

Cameo (bad mark probably where a price sticker covered preventing natural aging color to develop). $10.00 – 15.00.

Box shown open — note holes pierced on both lid and side of bottom half. After hanging it somewhere convenient, I wonder if the owner might have used this for holding cufflinks, spare change, or ear "bobs"? $10.00 – 15.00.

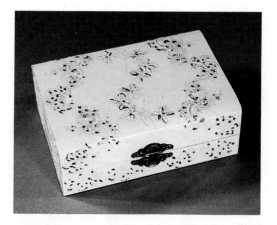

The top and front of this 5½" x 8" box is decorated with a floral repoussé design accentuated by dots of gilt here and there. Although the pattern is the same on all sides, it is only accentuated with gilt paint on the top and front. It is lined with red silk carefully tucked into pleats on the inside of the lid. The base is shaped to hold shaving brush, razor, and something else in front as well as the soap mug which is decorated with violets and shiny gold. The bottom has a painted gold "S." $35.00 – 45.00.

A select group of boxes in the closed and open position, some with treasures stored inside. $5.00 – 45.00 each.

Two woven boxes. The smaller one has a plain molded lid of thin celluloid. $6.00 – 12.00 each.

Ring boxes. Left: This particular round box is marked "Dennison" on the bottom. The bottom part is covered in light-colored velvet with a slot to hold the ring. The lid has a satin circle printed: W. Wilson, Jeweler, 1011 Broadway, Oakland, CAL. (California). This particular box has slots cut up part way on each side to the double indentation lines for some unknown reason. $15.00 – 20.00. I saw a box identical to this drum-shaped box with slightly domed top that was labeled "Thimble Box" and contained a silver and gold thimble ($55.00). Thimbles were often given as a reward for completing a needlework course or "sampler." The right-hand ring box is square with a hinge on one side. It also has a slot to hold a ring. $20.00 – 25.00.

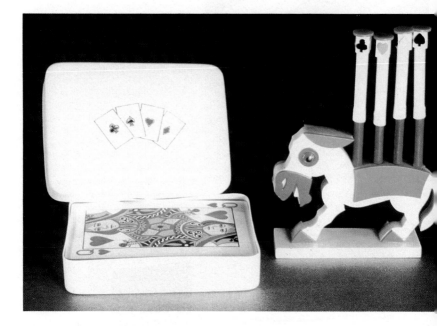

Card Box with suits arranged clubs, spades, hearts, and diamonds. This is an unu
order of arrangement of suits. $6.00 – 10.00. Short pencils topped with celluloid
decorations and little flat orange tops are inserted into the back of a cutout don
with orange celluloid applied eyes, mouth, saddle, hoofs, and gigantic ears. Gua
teed to make you smile, even if you are losing! $12.00 – 20.00.

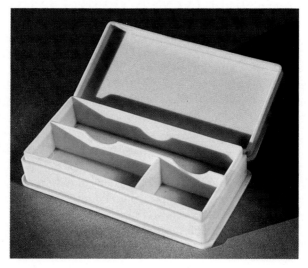

is box may have n designed espe-ly to hold "game ces." $25.00 – 0.

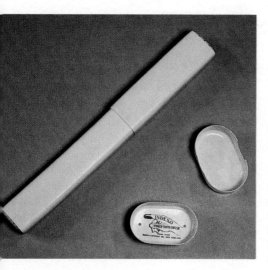

This looks like a rather standard and currently manufactured toothbrush holder with pierce-work on both ends. However, this one is made of celluloid. The two pieces telescope down to about 3". $6.00 – 10.00. When opened, the smaller box reveals a surprise. The printing says "Indexo - the finger tooth brush" with an illustration of using your index finger as the "handle." Alas, it was empty except for the printing. The bottom half also has two holes for draining any excess moisture. $8.00 – 12.00.

BUTTONS AND BUTTONHOOKS

Both buttons and buttonhooks have a following of collectors know far more than I do about this subject. Again, the mate (celluloid) has such a versatility of shapes and contours availa in a variety of buttons. I had a little fun laying out the buttonhooks – agai assorted shapes and sizes – for the basic tic-tac-toe and filling in the sp with some of the buttons and buckles in my collection. In general, I h single buttons but whenever possible I purchase a pair to use as earrings.

I will have to leave it to the expert button and buttonhook collector give a true value to these items. Instead of being $1.00 to $4.00 as a too buttonhook might be marked to $18.00 and it might have that value to a lector of that specific item. I would believe that even a buttonhook colle would devalue if the item were rusty, stained, or bent.

For my collection the value of buttons would not exceed $2.00 each I would only pay $18.00 for a combination buttonhook and shoe horn.

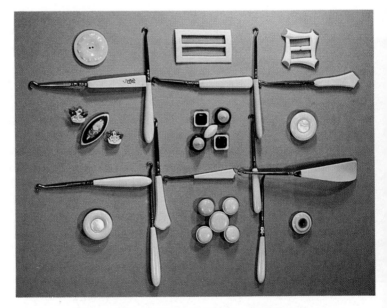

Button, $.50 – 2.00. Button hooks, $6.00 – 18.00.

CALENDAR

Have you had experience using a perpetual calendar? Sometimes they are found in the miscellaneous pages of telephone directories. To explain: there are 14 basic years that are assigned numbers. There is an index with the year you wish to select. The practical use of this might be the following scenario. A supplier of calendars is overstocked for a particular year. 1987 for example might be advertised for use in 1998. Or if you are really frugal — as I believe our forefathers were — you might find that you had not used a diary or executive notebook in 1981. It also would be good in 1998 without crossing out anything but the year!

The perpetual calendar shown is on the same principle except it is for a year — any year. The names of two months with a row of days of the week face top and bottom on six pieces of celluloid. These month cards are slightly larger than the pieces of celluloid with the days of the month with the 1st day beginning each day on a separate card: 1st on Monday, 1st on Tuesday, etc. All 13 of the cards fit into the stand or card holder with the current correct month in front. All month cards have 31 days on them. It would be up to the caretaker of the calendar to see that the new month was in place on the proper day. Really not too difficult!

Calendar, perpetual, copyrighted 1893, initial "D" in upper left corner; frame is sterling silver. $32.00 – 45.00.

CLOCKS

Each of the three clock faces are 2⅛" to 2¼" each althoug the 3 clocks are very dissimilar in size and shape. One is ⅛" tall with a 6¼" x 2⅝" base. The one with 9½" x 2" is 4¾ tall. The taller one is 6" tall with 4½" x 1⅞" base. This one has such beautiful gloss. Where the clocks used to be available for $15.00 t $25.00 they now are valued from $75.00 to $125.00.

These three keep very good time. No batteries to replace and n electricity to pay for but their tick-tock is so loud that they are not usu ally kept wound.

Clocks, $75.00 – 125.00.

DESK SETS

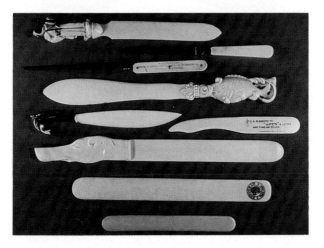

iscellaneous desk accessories $12.00 – 38.00.

om top to bottom: Letter opener, three-dimensional figure of a "wise man" or me man in a long flowing robe.

vo metal letter openers with celluloid handles. A real handful of a letter opener, a h entwined in seaweed, reverse of fish on the back.

small letter opener with gilt handle. 6" curved letter opener: t's a Pleasure to "Open" a letter and find an order. The Whitehead and Hoag Co. wark, N.J. 6/6/1905." On reverse side — Hugh N. Johnson Northwestern Repre- ntative The Whitehead and Hoag Co. Result Producing Adv. Novelties Phone ain 497 Seattle." All of it very readable except the tiny line on the "It's a Plea- re.." side.

page turner with whippet or greyhound head as the handle. The blade is tapered a portion of the sides but not at the tip.

very similar looking item: 1½" wide x 6 – 8" long stick with rounded corners with without markings of any kind might be a foam scraper to wipe the excess foam or ad off a beer. On one end there is this marking inside a double circle: KYNOCH d. and Trade Mark with strange design resembling a lion's head.

straight-edge to draw straight lines, but without measurements such as a ruler with ich we are familiar. Or perhaps a celluloid tongue depressor.

te: While visiting a shop in the Las Vegas area, I saw a very attractive straight ge piece of celluloid (approximately 1¼" x 7" with an ornate silver lacework pocket one end. The dealer told me that it was a Victorian ladies' "page turner" — "you ow these Victorian ladies did not wish to get ink on their hands or gloves" and was ing $65.00. When I asked where I might learn more about these page turners, I s referred to *Wilson's Victoriana*. Upon my return home I checked this book at my al library but I cannot confirm that this is true. A page turner would be pointed or nt (squared) on the end and tapered on each side. The opposite end (the end to held in the hand) might have some ornate decoration, yet be comfortable to hold he hand and this end would not be tapered on the sides.

Basic Desk Set in rusty-orange satin-lined leather case:
  Letter opener
  Point (to lift impressed wax seal from envelope)
  Scissors. Set $32.00 – 35.00.
  Business card holder, with dress cutter's card. $15.00 – 17.00.
  Blotter. $10.00 – 15.00.
  Letter holder. $15.00 – 27.00.
  Pencil sharpener, figural. $32.00 – 35.00.

Letter Holder, $15.00 – 27.00.

Blotter, $10.00 – 15.00.

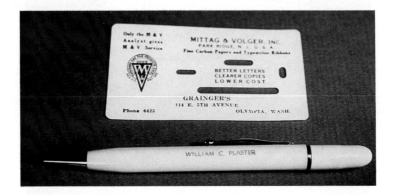

Mechanical pencil, $5.00 – 12.00. Guide for making manual corrections on a typed page, $3.00.

Pencil sharpener. Yes, this elephant has a purpose for being on the desk! $32.00 – 35.00.

DRESSER SETS

Some phraseology is very different now than in the late 1880s to early 1900s but since fruit shapes are consistent both then and now I chose to use terms that could have been used at the time of production. Actually, I'm sure that various sets had a precise name, but since I do not know these pattern names (and if I did would lack the background as to why this name was used) and keep it much simpler, I am providing the following KEY using names based on basic shapes:

1. Round
2. Square
3. Rectangle
4. Oval
5. Triangle

From a side view:
1. Straight
2. Apple-shaped or prominent shoulder
3. Evenly rounded — midline bulge (convex)
4. Pear-shaped the bulge is lower down
5. Concave, wider at the top and bottom than the middle
6. Flare, wider at top edge only
   Sub-shapes in addition to the basic side view

   a. Base
   b. Knob feet
      1. Round balls
      2. Oval balls
      3. Shaped

Lid Shapes:
1. Round
2. Square
3. Rectangle
4. Oval
5. Triangle

From a side view:
1. Flat
2. Slightly raised in center
3. Domed
4. Knob
5. Self-edge inside box
6. Self-edge outside box
7. Applied edge inside box

I kept thinking how exciting it would be to see an early catalog French Ivory sets when just before Christmas a new friend, dealer, and collector of celluloid covered albums and authority on celluloid boxes, And Behrendt, sent me a copy of a 1930 – 31 Catalog of "DuPont Accessories for the Boudoir." What a wonderful present! I read and reread every word!

Of particular interest to me was this paragraph: "Two distinctive new patterns have been added to the Pyralin line for 1930 — Lustris and Madlon...Lustris, with its gleaming satin-like surface on a crystal-like base, introduces an entirely new and striking effect."

Du Pont had introduced Lucite in 1928 and was adding four new patterns in boudoir accessories. They featured each of these new patterns on the first pages in the catalog plus other established patterns, all available in a variety of colors: Springtime Green, Peach Antoinette, Colonial Rose, Continental Blue, and Buff. (Did you ever hear such descriptive color names for the Du Pont Pyralin new patterns?)

The new Lustris pattern was available in Jade, Rose, and Maize in Satin Lustre-on-Crystal. It sold retail for $25 for a ten-piece set:

hair brush	shoe hook
comb	shoe horn
mirror	puff box (for loose
nail polisher (buffer)	powder)
cuticle knife	tray
nail file	jewel box
scissors	picture frame
	clock

A dealer could purchase 10 pieces for $15.50 and all 14 pieces for $27.? ($44 retail). Each was individually boxed and each "combination assemble in a container" which appeared to be a fitted, shaped cardboard box lined with satin draping. A three-piece set was mirror, comb, and hair brush.

Other Du Pont Pyralin patterns followed. Sonya emphasizes an octagon shape in Jade, Rose, Maize, and White Pearl-on-Amber with octagon tray and puff box and perfume bottle. Picture frame and clock were not shown in this pattern.

The Sheraton pattern on page 74 caught my interest. This pattern was "One of the first toiletware patterns ever created based on a true period design. It was inspired by the work of that famous craftsman whose name it bears — Sheraton." It was available in White, Goldenglow, and Jade Pearl-on-Amber. Several extra pieces were available in this pattern—in fact a total of 20 pieces! Consumer Price $100.00! My piece would be a Goldenglow Pearl-on-Amber puff or vanity box, originally priced $5.00 retail, 1930 – 31 (See pages 135 and 136.)

DU PONT ACCESSORIES
FOR THE BOUDOIR
Lucite .... *Pyralin*

Catalog
for
1930-31

DU PONT VISCOLOID COMPANY, Inc.
Main Sales Office: 530 Fifth Avenue, New York City
Factory: Arlington, New Jersey

BOSTON, 38 Chauncy Street
CHICAGO, North American Building
SAN FRANCISCO, 745 Mission Street

CANADIAN REPRESENTATIVE
Canadian Industries Limited
Montreal, Canada

PRICES SUBJECT TO CHANGE WITHOUT NOTICE

Du Pont
Boudoir
Accessories

DUPONT

A radical departure is the branding of the lowest price sets with the du Pont oval and the group named Arlton, thus bringing to bear the force of all du Pont advertising to the entire line of du Pont toiletware.

Whether it is a Lucite, Pyralin or Arlton set, it has been designed by experts who thoroughly understand modern style trends. In the 1930 du Pont line there is a pattern and a color to harmonize with every style of interior decoration. There is a price for every purse. Each set is branded with the famous du Pont oval—which years of consistent national advertising have taught the consumer to accept as a seal of honesty, fine workmanship and generous value.

We believe therefore that this year's line is the most attractive and most saleable that we have ever offered to the trade. Even the gift boxes, which have become such a determining factor in the sale of toiletware, have been redesigned to display each individual pattern and color to the best advantage, in order to make the merchandise the most appealing and most desirable.

Concentrate on the du Pont line. It gives you the most advanced styling, a complete style and price range, easier selling and reduced investment.

The NEW du Pont
Boudoir Accessories

WITH the introduction of Lucite in 1928, du Pont started an entirely new vogue in boudoir accessories. The new Lucite creations which were brought out the following year spread this vogue rapidly until there is today a growing demand for carefully styled, quality toiletware, truly appropriate for the boudoirs of today.

This year again, du Pont introduces many new features which will more firmly establish this new vogue.

The four new Lucite patterns represent a distinct advance in the toiletware art. Adam is reminiscent of one of the finest art periods of old England; Fleuret combines the dash and spontaneity of the French with the American idea of modernism; Trianon is truly feminine in the Louis XVI manner, with its long graceful mirror and its exquisite green and peach colors; and Monticello contains those same style elements which are so highly prized today in rare glass, china, silver and other art objects of the American Colonial period.

Two distinctive new patterns have been added to the Pyralin line for 1930— Lustris and Madelon. Both are priced for quick turnover and designed to appeal to that great mass market which represents the big volume in toiletware. Lustris, with its gleaming satin-like surface on a crystal-like base, introduces an entirely new and striking effect.

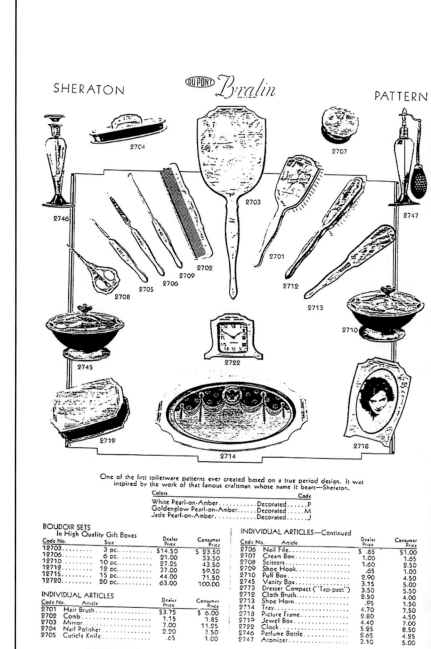

SHERATON   **DUPONT** *Bralin*   PATTERN

One of the first toiletware patterns ever created based on a true period design. It was inspired by the work of that famous craftsman whose name it bears—Sheraton.

Colors		Code
White Pearl-on-Amber	Decorated	P
Goldenglow Pearl-on-Amber	Decorated	M
Jede Pearl-on-Amber	Decorated	J

BOUDOIR SETS
In High Quality Gift Boxes

Code No.	Size	Dealer Price	Consumer Price
12703	3 pc.	$14.50	$ 23.50
12706	6 pc.	21.00	33.50
12710	10 pc.	27.25	43.50
12712	12 pc.	37.00	59.50
12715	15 pc.	44.00	71.50
12720	20 pc.	63.00	100.00

INDIVIDUAL ARTICLES

Code No.	Article	Dealer Price	Consumer Price
2701	Hair Brush	$3.75	$ 6.00
2702	Comb	1.15	1.85
2703	Mirror	7.00	11.25
2704	Nail Polisher	2.20	3.50
2705	Cuticle Knife	.65	1.00

INDIVIDUAL ARTICLES—Continued

Code No.	Article	Dealer Price	Consumer Price
2706	Nail File	$ .65	$1.00
2707	Cream Box	1.00	1.65
2708	Scissors	1.60	2.50
2709	Shoe Hook	.65	1.00
2710	Puff Box	2.90	4.50
2745	Vanity Box	3.15	5.00
2773	Dresser Compact ("Top-pact")	3.50	5.50
2712	Cloth Brush	2.50	4.00
2713	Shoe Horn	.95	1.50
2714	Tray	4.70	7.50
2718	Picture Frame	2.80	4.50
2719	Jewel Box	4.40	7.00
2722	Clock	5.25	8.50
2746	Perfume Bottle	2.65	4.25
2747	Atomizer	3.10	5.00

BE SURE TO ADD CODE LETTER OF DESIRED COLOR TO CODE NUMBER OF EACH SET OR ARTICLE ORDERED

[21]

Another page shows the Mayflower pattern, White, Rose, or Jade Pearl-a-Amber. Basic set of 10 pieces, dealer price $22.50, consumer price $46.00. All 20 pieces, consumer $80.00. A glass bottom perfume tray is shown with a pictorial of three maids dancing. The shape of this pattern is familiar to me. It has a gentle domed edge which is repeated on the mirror, brush, jewel box, clock, picture frame, and tray. The perfume tray however, is very different in basic shape and the center of the tray is made of glass which resists stains. A small cream box is shown. I would bet it has glass-liner even though it cost the dealer only 55 cents. Many pieces in my collection have this basic shape.

One page lists more "Boudoir Accessories" not really distinguishing the Lucite patterns from the Pyralin patterns except that an earlier page had listed Trianon and Monticello as Lucite patterns and Madelon as a new Pyralin pattern. The prices were the major clue: the Pyralin pattern Madelon was $7.00 (dealer) for a 3 piece set "in Fancy Gift Boxes" where the Lucite ranges from a low of $9.35 to $12.50 for 3 pieces. Ten pieces of Pyralin, $12.50 and 10 pieces of Lucite Trianon, $21.00.

And so it seems I should amend my vernacular to puff box not powder box, nail polisher not buffer, and accessories for the boudoir rather than dresser sets. It was especially interesting to see what composed a set. Where do all these other pieces fit in? What were they used to hold?

These new colors and shapes were no doubt developed with the conviction that the consumer wished a change from the original ivory color and basic shapes so more and more choices were made available.

I do know what I prefer. I like a translucent blown piece with a high gloss with lots of striations. Although I see them referred to as "even striations," my preference is for the pieces where the striations vary in width to accentuate the shape and in closer imitation of natural ivory. This would occur when the pressure would stretch the plastic material into the curves forcing the spacing to spread into an attractive pattern. This spread would be similar but not identical on the opposite side of the object and often the lid would match the grain of the piece. How this was managed I am not sure! The accompanying piece would be similar in color and striations.

Even though I have many pieces that look very similar in color and size, the lids are not interchangeable. From one piece of a set to the matching piece, the lids are not interchangeable. It is as if every piece is individually made rather than a product of a manufacturers assembly line!

Basic Dresser Set

This is a basic dresser set. The major pieces are marked "IVOF DU BARRY PY-RA-LIN." These items each have in common domed or convex curve with a smaller concave area on each sid If the item is round, this convex/concave pattern results in a total of four convex curves.

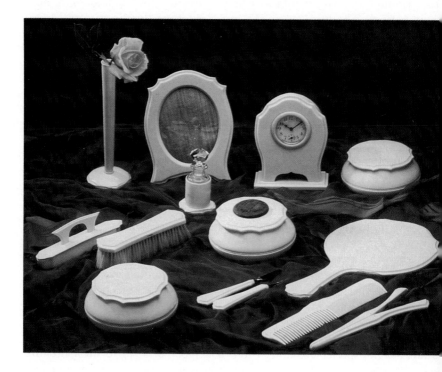

ack row left to right:

. A vase, with dome-shaped base, for that freshly picked blossom or a few dried owers. The four convex curve pattern appears around the base. The upright ortion is a slightly tapered tube and since it is watertight, does not need to be ned.

. The picture frame is shown without picture to exhibit the richly-hued olive elvet which lines the inside of the frame as well as the back and easel. The lass is slightly curved. The horned tips between the convex and concave areas re modified and elongated in this item to form the feet of the frame.

. The top of the clock matches the shape of the frame but the feet are firmly ttached to a rectangle base rather than free-standing like the picture frame. The mall round clock is mounted in the center of the upper half with the usual set-ng knobs in the back. With its loud tick and alarm, it keeps one aware of the assing of time.

. A powder box with the same four convex curve pattern and slightly domed lid. he bottom portion is pear-shaped with a double line of indentation near the ottom which curves under, seamless inside and out.

. The nail buffer is at the left of the middle row. This is a traditional well-known nd well-used item.

. A long narrow brush is topped with a shape similar to the top of the buffer. A mall convex curve is centered on each end with smaller concave curves on ither side of it. The sides of this elongated rectangle are ever so slightly con-ave. The bristles are quite stiff and I would judge that it might be used as a lothes brush, rather than a hair brush (which I neglected to include in this rouping). Check the upper left of the photo at the top of page 78.

. The delicate perfume bottle holder has a base matching the vase. This rather rdinary bottle boasts a brilliantly cut glass stopper.

. Although resembling a hair-receiver, at closer look you will note that the box in he very center of the picture is actually a very worn pincushion. Again, it has the our convex curve edge. Its most unique feature is on the underside of the lid: a ound mirror in excellent condition.

. A hand mirror is at the far right of this middle row. Again you will see the hape of the frame and clock repeated around the mirror only this time the elon-ation is into a handle which ends in the concave, convex, concave shape.

0. The row in the front has another powder box. How many boxes actually elong in a set is a mystery to me, especially since this group came to me as eparates.

1. I have included two fingernail tools with the basic shape at the end of their andles.

2. The hand hold of this large comb has the basic shape.

3. And finally on the far right front row: a glove stretcher! While the handle is queezed, it makes a shape matching the mirror handle, brush, and buffer as well as he fingernail implements. I like to think that this group is like a family that started ogether and then went separate ways and now is once more united in my collection.

BRUSHES

See how they vary in size and shape! $6.50 – 15.00.

Fingernail brush. $8.00 – 12.00.

Shaving brushes (one with case with single drain hole in bottom), $10.00 – 35.00. Ordinary shaving brushes of varying shapes and color of bristles, $8.00 – 12.50. Hat brush with long soft bristles for brushing that beaver hat or is it a barber's brush to clear away those just-cut stray hairs? $20.00 – 25.00. Thin compact traveler's brush in genuine leather case with snap closure; imprint: "Patented July 26th, 1910" on one side and "Travelers" (script) with "France" printed underneath. $32.00 – 35.00. Baby brush with very soft bristles. $6.00 – 8.00.

COMBS

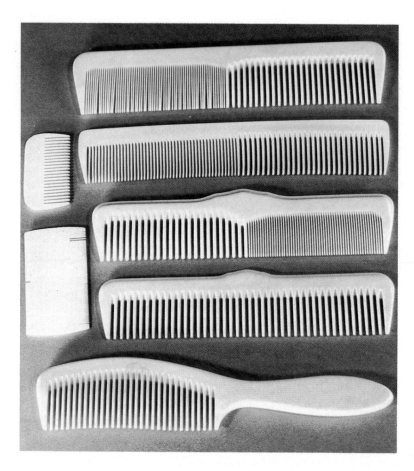

Assorted sizes and shapes, including comb with handle. This shape was a great surprise to me — it looks so modern! $3.00 – 15.00.

FINGERNAIL POLISHERS AND BUFFERS

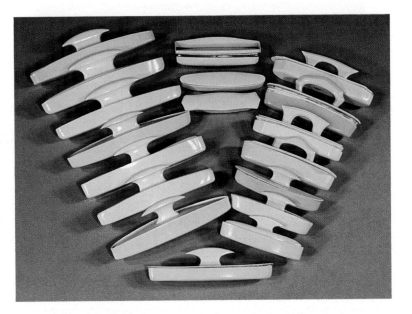

This photo gives you an opportunity to compare the variations in color within the creamy ivory group. You will note that the majority have a simi-lar wedge-shaped piece attached at right angles in the center of the top, yet almost every one is slightly different in size and shape. It is almost as if, although this was a manufactured product, each item was given a certain amount of individual hand assembly and finishing. The one at the bottom of the picture in the center is very squared and rough cut. It looks as though it was sawed from a flat piece and left without any buffing or shap-ing. Without tray $1.00 – 3.00. With tray $4.50 – 7.00.

The three at center top of the picture do not have an attached handle. They are still comfortable to hold and use. Top center, the base of the buffer pivots and becomes the handle, as shown. (Close-up shown on page 82.)

Other than the previous three exceptions, the rest of the stack look similar to each other and to this picture of one alone with a Danish coin. This buffer was purchased in a flea market in Denmark. It is exactly like the others of this type. 6 Kroner (approx $1.00.)

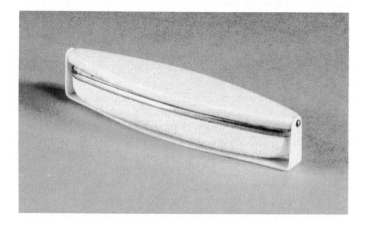

Buffer with pivoting handle. Shown with base in place. Unusual. $6.00 – 8.00.

FINGERNAIL FILES

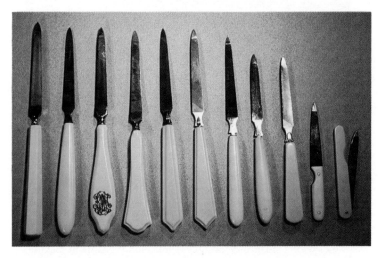

Another implement well-used over many years! $3.00 – 8.00 each.
Available in various sizes and shapes including a folding one on the
right end. I know I do not have to explain how to use a fingernail file!

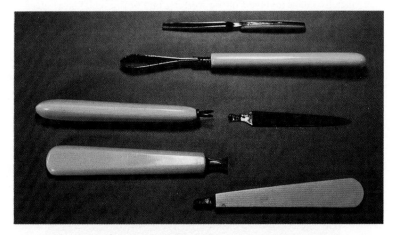

I would like to explain that some file holders seem to have been made to replace
the file. You will see in this photo that there is a file with a short extension in the
center of the picture. This would slip into the handle and be held in place by a
pair of grippers composed of two short pieces of metal which are a part of the
handle. Dealers have tried to sell me these handles with the grippers only
attached. I have been told that these were tweezers. No way! At the top of the
picture you will see two styles of real tweezers. (Yes, I know I'm the one who
purchased "artichoke" dishes and later learned that they were really just individual serving plates with the cups missing — but listen up dealers — you can't fool
me about everything!)

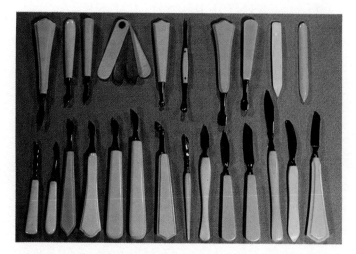

An assortment of tools from fingernail scrapers, cuticle pushers, a tool with a small pierced hole, short emery boards in a celluloid cover, and other sharp and pointy and sometimes vicious-looking tools. Handles were sometimes made of bone while other pieces in the same set were made of celluloid. There was usually metal involved in the working end of the tool. Occasionally the entire tool was made of celluloid as the two in the right end of the upper row. Tweezers $5.00 – 8.00. Other tools $3.00 – 6.00.

Fingernail Scissors — note the ones shaped to match sets. $6.00 – 15.00.

FINGERNAIL CASES AND TOOLS

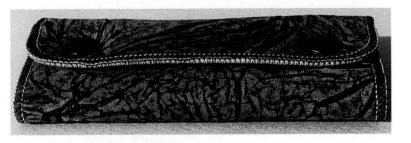

A nice small (approx. 4" long) green leather case with a very flat buffer, a pushing tool, tool for cleaning under the fingernail, an all metal file, and one empty space for an unknown tool. The lining is a brilliant red. Pink and white ribbons are held in place with metal staples to form web pockets to hold each tool. This case is in like-new condition and even though one tool is missing, present day kits similar to this one often sell for $25.00.

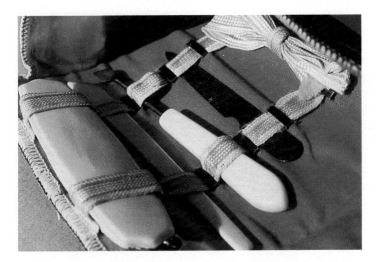

In stark contrast, this leather case has seen better days. It is brittle from sun exposure and lack of lanolin. The inside is sun faded in areas. Although years ago it may have been an attractive bright color now it has faded unevenly to a pale hue. It does have a number of tools in good condition, even though several slots are empty. The basic pushers, buffer, emery boards and cover, celluloid pomade box, etc. make this a steal at $25.00 even if the case were to be tossed away.

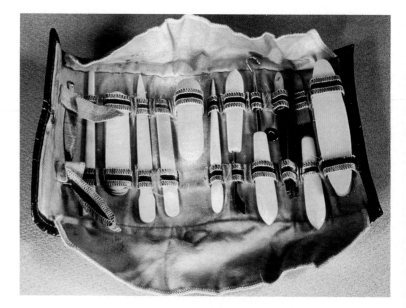

This is a large, very complete set in a black embossed leather case in very good condition. It has rouge or polishing compound boxes, a shoe horn, a nail file in good condition — every necessary tool is included. I purchased this for $32.00 (admittedly a bargain). I would set its value at $65.00 – 85.00.

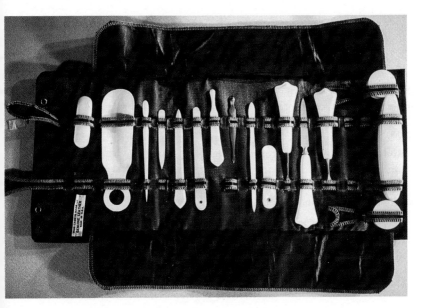

POWDER PUFF BOXES AND HAIR RECEIVER

I have a dresser set that I cherish that was given to me by a maid lady. She was very progressive for her time — the early 20s. S called the drayman to pick up her trunk at the family home a transport it in the dray to another city where she was to work as bookkeep She had wonderful stories of her working years. One lucky day after she h opened the incoming mail, she found a loose diamond on the desk. H boss thought it an impossible task to locate the owner so she was allowed keep it.

I'm sure she was very good at her job. One day she was asked to co pete with a newly invented calculator. She won! As an end-of-year bon her boss gave her $25.00. She took it and bought a dresser set of pyralin. S took such good care of it that when she gave it to me almost 50 years later. had very little evidence of use although it was used daily. She had a spec powder with which she would polish the set. Even the bottoms of t pieces had very few scratches.

It speaks very well for the care that this wonderful lady gave her dres set that it was without blemish considering that this material did have shortcomings. It was actually very fragile. It not only scratched easily, b also dented, stained, and melted. Aside from that (or because of its m leability) it could be molded in a form, poured into sheet molds and form sawed, and planed. It was relatively nonporous and it did look like iv with its varying striations. It was very light which makes it even more am ing that it is said that over 40,000 tons of it was produced during the cell loid years.

Then there is the very common hair receiver. I am always amazed at t number of people who have no idea what this item was designed to ho Although we may not see anyone today saving every strand of hair th appears in their comb and brush and painstakingly braiding it into a ha piece to add to their coiffure to fill out that thinning appearance, it d make one realize that this is something more we have in common with c ancestors — pride in appearance and the inevitable thinning of the hair w age! Now one has a choice of applying a chemical or adding strands matching hair, called thatching or hair transplanting plugs of one's own h from thicker areas, and using the hair receiver to hold cotton balls.

In the past, another use for hair was to make watch fobs and pieces th were kept inside lockets and picture frames as keepsakes.

The basic shapes of the round puff box, using the key on page 69
>From a side view:
Straight
Apple-shaped or prominent shoulder
Evenly rounded, midline bulge (convex)
Pear-shaped, the bulge is lower down

Unless otherwise noted, all those shown are flat on the bottom without feet or added bases of any kind.

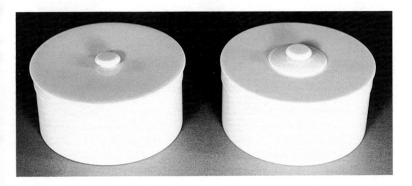

Round, straight sides, little flat-topped knobs on lid for the receiver lid. Yes, you read that correctly! A lid for the receiver lid is an unusual feature and deserves an extra expenditure. It was many years before I saw my first lid for a lid. The contents are better protected and are out of sight. $22.50 – 25.00.

Refer back to the key on page 69 to refresh your memory until you can follow easily. First number refers to the basic shape, second number to the side view shape, etc. Round (1), straight sides (1), flat round lid with four convex curves at the edge with small concaves between the convex. The lids are quite thick and perfectly flat. The lids overlap the bottom of the boxes and fit very firmly and snugly. Marked: Ivory Pyralin (in a curve) over DUBARRY. $15.00 – 20.00.

Round, straight sides, round lid is domed in the center and have six (6) convex curves around the edge. There are sharp little points between the convex curves which I call horns. The lid is slightly domed and although this box contained a powder puff, it has a hole in the center. There is a thin platform that has been shaped into two widths applied to form the bottom of the box. The small box has a screw on lid and does fit in the hole but the hole is not tapered as if it was really meant to hold this little box. The bottom and sides of the little box were molded as one piece. Both boxes, although of different shapes and construction were sold together and match in color and gloss. Only the larger box has a mark: top line IVORY, middle line tall on each end in stylized letters ACWALITE, bottom line in caps FRENCH DESIGN. $12.00 – 18.00. It also has other marks that someone has added in green ink or paint: 1634 and what looks like "uua" in script. The numbers 335 have been scratched below the other writing in the bottom.

Round, straight sides, round slightly domed tops, six convex curves around the edge with sharp little points between the curves. This set has three matching pieces. They are three different sizes and there are different markings on the sides but all are double indented lines, but the middle sized box has two sets of double indented lines. The largest box is the hair receiver and has a thin platform applied bottom. I use platform to mean that it protrudes beyond the sides. $20.00 – 25.00.

Round (1), rounded apple-shape (2), lid round (1), slightly raised (2), and knob (4). Both pieces are blown in a mold. There are obvious seam marks on the sides of both pieces. No marks. $12.00 – 15.00.

Another 1, 2, 1, 2, with 4. (Can you follow this on the key using the numbers only?) Marked: Ivory Py-ra-lin in an oval configuration with oval shape drawn. $12.00 – 15.00.

There are actually three sets of two in the above combination. The pieces are not interchangeable. The set and slope of the shoulders are slightly different. There are definite "sets" that belong together in color, exact shape, and matching or compatible striation patterns. $12.00 – 15.00.

The third set! Marked "Ivory Pyralin" in one straight line. $12.00 – 15.00.

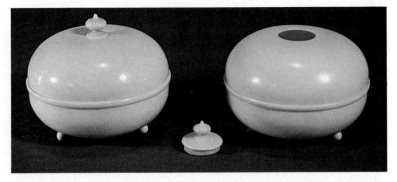

Using the key: 1 (round), 3 (midline bulge), sub b (knob feet), 2 (oval balls), lid 1 (round), 3 & 4 (domed and knob). No mark. $20.00 – 25.00.

Again using the key: 1 round, 3 evenly rounded, midline budge, 1 lid round, 3 domed, 4 with knob upright oval, bottom domed in the opposite direction. Marked: Ivory Pyralin in one straight line. $22.50 – 25.00.

My favorite little set, on an oval tray: 1 round, 3 evenly rounded, tops are blown into a dome matching the blown bottom halves and have 6-self-edge outside the bottom half of box. No marks. Everything about this set appeals to me. It has wonderful gloss and wonderful striation variations. It is very smooth to the touch. $25.00 – 30.00 plus sentimental value.

This begins the examples of the 4th side view of the basic round shape in the key, otherwise known as pear-shaped. The next three sets are 1 (round), 4 (pear-shaped — the bulge is further down), the lids are 1 (round), 2 (slightly raised to flat). The mark on the puff box is arranged in dome shape: Ivory Py-ra-lin and straight across bottom: DUBARRY (there is no additional line around the words). The hair receiver has a lid. For something less than 2" wide, it has the an immense amount of construction: the knob is slightly raised in the center and tapers down to a smaller base which is attached probably by glue to a disk that just fits the opening in the hair receiver. The disk has a perfectly round ring attached to the bottom of it to fit it securely into the hole in the receiver. All of these pieces have striations that match perfectly with each other and the striations on the main lid of the receiver. This piece marked: "Ivory Py-ra-lin" inside oval plus 464/267. Both lids are mold-blown with hollow space into the edge that overlaps the lower piece and also forms the edge which extends down into the base. 15.00 – 20.00 per set.

Same basic shape with initial "D" on all pieces. The two smaller pieces have a different profile: 1 (round), straight to flare with a definite base or rounded platform. The lids are slightly raised and have a rolled self-edge over the lower half of box. Only the large puff box has a Ivory Pyralin Dubarry mark inside a well-marked oval, on bottom of box. $18.00 – 20.00, set.

This pear-shaped pair is oversized — the largest I have ever seen. The mark is five pointed star in the center of the bottom. No knobs. Truly dramatic in siz 6½" across. The 5" lids are larger than most standard size sets! Unusual. $25.00 30.00, set.

Again using the key: 1 (round), 6 (flare-shaped), 1 (base) rounded platform; lid 1 (round), 2 (slightly raised in center), 7 applied edge outside lower half of box. $18.00 – 20.00, set.

1 (round), 6 (flare-shaped), self-bulge near bottom, 1 piece blown construction. Marked "Colonial Quality" with strange little drawing on left of words which could be a sheaf of wheat. $6.00.

The two pieces of this set look like they match perfectly. The pieces are alike in color and texture but if they ever were together in the past they have been apart for many years before I got them together again. The short one has a puff or padding in the bottom. The hair receiver flares outward slightly toward the top and has slight shoulders. Both lids are slightly raised toward the center and overlap the bottom half. Marked: Germany. Very thin celluloid. No striations. Pale off-white. $9.00 – 12.00 each piece.

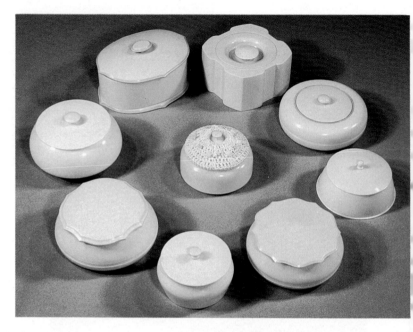

Assorted sizes and shapes of boxes without a matching hair receiver or other bo $10.00 – 25.00 each. You might note that in the center of this group of boxe there is one with a crocheted lid cover. There is one basically square box. It very unusual. It is shown alone in the trademark section on page 25. The botto is applied or glued onto the sides. The sides are double thickness. While you se the almost four-leaf clover shape outside, the inside is smoothly round witho seam except for where the bottom and top are attached. Even the lid is doub and nothing protrudes above the upper edge. There is a depression and the fl knob is attached in the center of the bottom of the depression so it is very ea to lift the lid by the knob. There is a tiny lip which prevents the lid from fallir into the opening. The striations on the lid and the striations on the top of th box can be lined up to match exactly. The unusual shape and construction this box would warrant a much higher value to any collector. Each item in th group is unique. Continuing clockwise: the short flat look, although the openir is standard size. The next one makes me want to sing "I'm a little teapot..." b it does not have a handle nor a spout. Standard pear-shape with convex an horned lid. Center bottom is a very small apple-shaped. Continuing clockwis another pear-shaped with covex/concave lid; another pear-shaped though mo rounded. To finish the circle: another very unusual box. This one is basicall oval with slight horns on both lid and platform in the center of the ends ar sides. A pale pink stripe outlines the knob and lid.

Square boxes with round very slightly domed lids. These were obviously blown in molds. No seams are visible. $20.00 – 25.00, set.

Assorted sizes and shapes of hair receivers without matching puff boxes. There is one very good example of a perfect flare shape center left. Does anyone have a partner for these pieces? $10.00 – 20.00, each.

One very beautiful hair receiver. $12.00 – 18.00. It is very light in color and has round knob feet. The other similar set shown on the bottom of page 93 has sharp little oval pill-shaped feet. This one is marked England on the bottom.

MIRRORS

I'm delighted that the DuPont catalog confirms that a hand mirror was considered a basic piece of every dresser set. Over the years these items were well used and suffered their share of stains and scratches. It is always a nice surprise to find one in very good condition. Sometimes the mirrors are still excellent and sometimes they are hazy and discolored. Prices would vary according to the condition not only of the celluloid surface but of the condition of the mirror itself. Often the mirror is an extremely desirable item to purchase alone and prices range from $15.00 to $32.00, depending on condition. (Also depending on whether the dealer wishes to continue to use this item in the booth as a sales tool, it may be NFS = not for sale.)

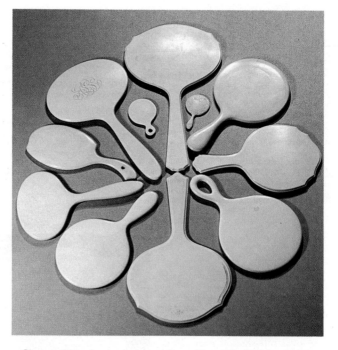

Group of hand mirrors, sized from 3" to 15". $6.00 – 35.00.

Purse mirrors, $8.00 – 15.00. Compacts, $6.00 – 35.00.

My favorite compact is the small-est one with a mirrored front which lifts to reveal a tiny powder puff with tiny pink ribbon. Note the hinge and simple delicate lift-ing tab opposite the hinge. The entire compact is very lightweight and made of very thin celluloid. $25.00. Next to this attractive and delicate item, the compact marked "Fuller" is totally clunky. The mirror is inside. The small comb fits in a totally utilitarian back pocket. It is sturdy and would hold powder and a puff. I show them together for contrast in esthetics. $10.00 – 12.50.

TRAYS

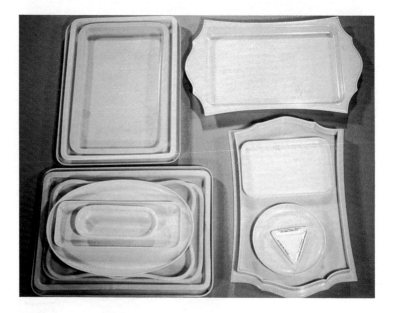

Trays. $2.00 – 8.00, each.

I couldn't resist showing you as many sizes and shapes as possible in the smallest possible area! Not quite "when you've seen one tray — you've seen them all," but they are pretty basically flat on the bottom and turned up on the edge all the way around! Some gently taper upward, some have an applied edge that reaches toward the sky then levels off in a horizontal lip. Others actually attempt to match a set of other pieces in basic shape (yes, we're into that convex/concave stuff again!). The tray is often the one piece of an entire set which has caught that drop of perfume or other liquid which permanently discolors it. Even worse, it is sometimes used as an ashtray. You can imagine what that does to the surface of this highly flammable material! Yes, I have been very deceptive in this photo and managed to cover the blemishes. If you were purchasing you might find these trays under a matching or compatible dresser set for $1.00 to $5.00 each. Note the oval under the small blown round powder box and receiver in the Dresser Sets section in the bottom photo on page 94. Each is incomplete without the other, in my opinion, and my favorite set. It is the set always closest to my heart and probably similar to the set given me by my grandmother long ago — before my conscious memory of loving and collecting items of this material. Perfume tray — see page 136. What a good idea to have the bottom surface made of glass or mirror to resist any perfume drips that would otherwise stain the celluloid! This one appears to have lace sandwiched between two layers of glass.

FANS

Fans were very popular in the 1700s. As a result of a high society ball given by Charles X at the Tuileries in 1829, fans were reintroduced to the ladies of the court and artisans all over Europe began to make fans again. The high-fashion fans of the eighteenth century were folding fans constructed in two different ways. A mount or leaf of pleated material, such as paper, fabric, or thin leather had sticks inserted or a single layer of the mount material was attached to one side of the sticks.

The fans in my collection are of the alternate construction. There is no mount. Celluloid sticks or blades are wide enough to overlap with those on either side forming the fan itself when open. Ribbon running from one blade to the next holds the fan together. This type of fan is called the brisé fan. The sticks or blades have identical elaborate pierced-work designs.

Both types have two outer guards which are thicker and wider than the other blades in order to protect the fan when it is folded. All the blades are fastened together at one end with a rivet or pin. Often a small loop or bale extends in the opposite direction of the blades and is held by the same rivet. A ribbon and perhaps a tassel is attached by which to carry the fan.

I have seen celluloid fans with fluffy ostrich feathers mounted on the end of each blade. I have also seen celluloid fans made with a mount of organdy, but both were in very poor condition since the mount was too delicate to have lasted through the years.

In the nineteenth and early twentieth centuries debutante fans were popular accessories for coming-out balls in England and America. Celluloid was a very good substitute for pierced ivory and mother-of-pearl blades and would make this very popular item affordable to many.

2½" brisé fan. $5.00 – 6.00. 6" brisé fan. $8.00 – 22.50. I have also included in m
picture a mechanical type fan with three blades. A push of the plunger separate
the blades and sends them whirling. The plunger returns to the out position to b
pressed inward again creating a breeze with very little effort. This has an actio
similar to a sparking toy with which I was familiar as a child. $12.50 – 15.00.

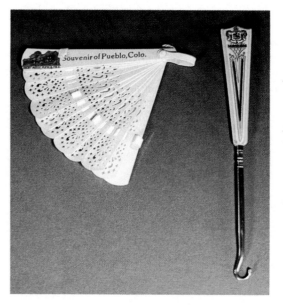

The fan made a very goo
souvenir item whe
imprinted with locatior
$6.00 – 10.00. I include
another souvenir in the pic
ture: a buttonhook fror
Hawaii — no doubt onl
used by a little old missior
ary on Sunday. $6.00
10.00.

JEWELRY

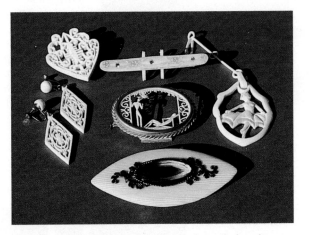

A group of jewelry pieces illustrating relative sizes.

I was surprised to find pearls and brilliants, gem stones and gold used in combination with the celluloid pieces. According to *Twenti-eth Century Fashionable Plastic Jewelry* by Lillian Baker (Collector Books, 1992) the first celluloid piece of jewelry was a bar pin handmade by George Berkander, circa 1909, "to be worn at the collar or neckline of a woman's garment, and sometimes used to join a detachable collar to the frock." It might have looked very much like the pin shown with swivel or tongue clip on the back and a brilliant imbeded in the front. Edges and corners were left very square, although not sharp to the touch. $6.00 – 8.00.

A very attractive pointe
oval of celluloid with stron
horizontal striations. An ova
opening has been cut and
very nice faceted blue topa
stone has been set in th
center with antique gol
bezel and a decorative lea
design extending at eac
end of the oval toward th
points. $25.00 – 45.00.

This is called a scarf pin.
There are two small loops of
celluloid (as shown better in
the shadow) to hold a scarf.
There are four raised flower-
shaped designs that have been
delicately painted and three
brilliants. I can see this appealing to a lady of an earlier era.
$12.50 – 15.00.

Two angular stylized figure
one standing, one loungin
surrounded by an oval an
twisted chain of gold. This is a
close as it gets to "the plac
cards that got away," the ones
didn't buy. I marvel at how th
piece survived as it is very del
cate and I'm sure there are li
tle pieces of the inset celluloi
that have been broken away i
putting this pin on or off. Th
catch has an extra little innova
tion; the piece you see extend
ing to the left must be pulle
outward to release the pir
$25.00 – 40.00.

This pin seems to be an advertising or commemorataive item. I'm not sure if this is a cherub or angel to which the modified safety pin is attached and from which the oyster-shell-shaped piece of celluloid hangs. The front says: "THE COUSINS" and under three pictures the names Virginia Dare, Pocahontas, and Minnehaha. Since Virginia Dare was the first English child born in America, perhaps these Native American Indians her cousins. The reverse side says: "Virginia Dare the first lady of our land extends you a welcome in her home under the big clock. Take Berkley Ferry in Norfolk, VA." Virginia Dare was born August 18, 1587, Roanoke Island. $25.00 – 28.00.

After the discovery of King Tutankhamen's tomb, many items of jewelry were designed after the scarab — the sacred beetle often depicted on carvings in the tomb. The pin and earrings shown were not purchased together. Each depicts the scarab and I find them compatible as a set. Earrings, $18.00. Pin, $18.00.

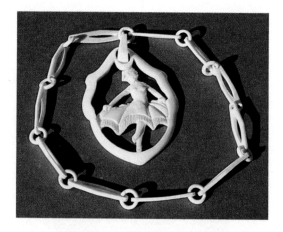

A dancing girl charm or pendant with short chain. $6.00 – 8.00.

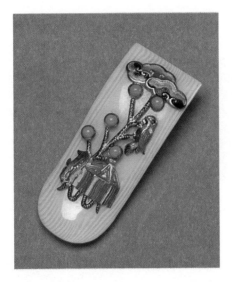

Again I was amazed at the workmanship and materials combined with celluloid. Although I like this material, I am used to people looking askance at something so close to plastic. This piece resembles cloisonné although cloisonné is thin strips of metal (called cloisons) soldered to a surface to form small cells or compartments which are then filled with colored enamel. I realize that it would not be possible to accomplish this on celluloid so the design would have been constructed and then attached to the celluloid. The colors are brilliant. The background of celluloid has a high gloss. I would not dare wear it for fear of losing it as the clip is not strong enough to hold anything together and even if just worn to be decorative it does not want to stay in place. The only safe place to clip it is in a jewelry box. But isn't it pretty? $40.00 – 65.00.

A necklace of 31 discs of graduating sizes. There is a hole in one edge of each disc through which a metal chain is strung. The clasp is barrel type with self threads. Very light and pleasant to wear. It is shown with a piece of clip jewelry which you may observe more closely above. $95.00 – 125.00.

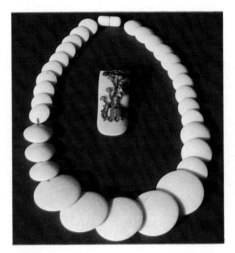

The cameo is created by carving shell or stone. The subject is usually a profile of a woman. The two cameos shown are frankly imitations of the real thing. They are press molded. $15.00 – 18.00, each.

Regardless of the problems that the owl has caused the northwest timber industry, this collection would not be complete without one. This owl came from Lulu's, Royal Oaks, Michigan. One eye is a bit different in color than the other — maybe he is just winking at us! He really did fly all the way from Detroit to Olympia — in my suitcase. $25.00 – 27.50.

Basket of flowers. Look closely and you will see that between the leaves and flowers a very thin transparent layer is left giving the whole design physical strength and unity. $10.00 – 15.00.

OBJETS D'ART

Shown are examples of several hollow blown pieces. These were no doubt made in molds as opposed to cut, planed, or molded in sheets. The birds are all hollow: canary and parrot and the swans in the foreground. One swan has wings that have been added to the basic shape by being attached at the forward edge for a lifelike appearance. The elephants, Scottie dog, and central figure are filled — probably with a plaster-of-Paris-like substance that adds weight and protection from being dented. All of the blown figures are very thin celluloid and because of their textured finish quite different in feel and appearance from the pieces in the back row. The glossy pieces in the back row are shown together because they are all upright, have weighted bases, and are designed to hold something. It may be disputed whether they are designed to hold a flower blossom, a hatpin, or a candle as might be suspected at least of the candleholder-shaped one on the left which is lined with tin. Knowing the flammability of this material, its use as a candleholder seems to be a very poor choice. One vase has a marble inside and I feel certain that this was not the original intent or design although it does add weight! However, at this time it is an integral part of the item as I have not been able to get it out!

Assorted vases. $12.50 – 22.50.
Hollow figures:
Canary. $8.00 – 15.00.
Parrot, on wood and wire stand. $12.00 – 15.00.
Swan. $20.00.
Swan, with applied wings. $25.00.
Horse, as is (repaired). $15.00.
Giraffe, small. $8.00 – 10.00.
Roly-poly. $100.00 – 150.00.
Scottie, filled (broken ear) if perfect. $27.50 – $35.00.
Elephants. $6.00 – 20.00 each.

Jackie Coogan, 7" tall on a thin 3¼" circular base. $65.00 – 185.00. One of the very special pieces in my celluloid collection is a figure of a young boy in ragged clothes with a three-sided box on a stick over his right shoulder. This is a representation of Jackie Coogan — first major child star. It shows him in oversize worn pants held up with suspenders, a ribbed knit top with a "Buster Brown" haircut sticking out from under a cloth cap with the bill pulled down over one ear, similar to the costume he wore in *The Kid* where his wistful waif role came close to stealing the show from Charlie Chaplin, then one of the greatest stars in film. This 1921 movie was his first of movie after movie in which Jackie Coogan was the child star. He was called the greatest boy actor in the world and was the #1 box office draw for Paramount Pictures. As with any collection, one thing leads to another. I had no idea that the history of old movies and early movie stars could be so interesting. I was really excited to find an autographed picture of the real little boy in a similar outfit. I have also discovered that there was a Jackie Coogan doll, cap and all. He was the first in a series of movie children to have a full page of paperdolls in costumes from several of his movies published in *Woman's Home Companion* in a 1925 issue and is given the credit for the law which regulates the earnings of minors and requires that at least 50% of a child's earnings is kept in trust for their future.

PERFUME BOTTLES

The perfume bottles in my collection vary greatly. They have one thing in common: each has a base made of celluloid! The base fits very snugly. It is as if the bottle was inserted sometime during the manufacturing process. I do not know that this is true. There does not seem to be any evidence that the bottle was attached by glue. The bottles themselves are all of clear glass. Each stopper is also unique. Some are frosted, some are faceted. I particularly recall admiring and then purchasing the one in the middle row that has the initials MAH. The three rounded bottles are each modified triangles. They fit snugly into this one round holder. The stoppers, beautifully faceted, vary slightly in height. As with other items of celluloid which combine with another material (in this instance, glass) there may be a value superceding that of the celluloid. I learned that some of the dresser sets with the bottom half made of glass, could have an additional value because of the rarity of the glass made by a specific manufacturer. I must apologize that I do not have the knowledge to take that into account in pricing. There are also the perfume bottle collectors, as well as bottle collectors who may influence the desirability of this item. $15.00 – 35.00 each.

PICTURES and FRAMES

What a nice gift for Mother! This is something I would give my mother: a verse and picture printed on celluloid. $125.00.

Three rectangular mirrors. $3.00 – 15.00.
Shirley Temple, Dionne Quintuplets, the original Narrows Bridge, Tacoma, Washington, each with its own special piece of history.

photograph of this darling little
irl with her curls and lacy dress
rinted on celluloid and in a 24 K.
old circled pin. She was actually
friend and acquaintance of my
other-in-law. After her death, I
as able to purchase this pin at
er estate sale as there was no
mily to treasure this piece. Ask-
g price $25.00. I will treasure
ou, Elgie. $22.50 – 25.00.

A very simple utilitarian frame, a rectangle with oval opening with glass to protect a photograph or perhaps just this old printed picture. $22.00 – 25.00.

Let me show you the back of th frame with its many features. Edg are applied on three sides of the bac The two sides are L-shaped for a fl piece of celluloid to slide into. Th bottom edge has a half-round tab keep the flat piece from slipping ou A leg is attached on the back to crea an easel. For stability the lower po tion of the leg is divided or split in two pieces from the base to about of the distance to the place attache A simple wire or pin allows this leg pivot outward. It can tip only as far allowed by the upper end whic pushes against the top portion of th back piece. Isn't that simple?

As well as the varying shapes and construction of each uniquely different frame, please look at the back of the picture frames at the bottom of the group of picture frames. Lower right corner is another view of the frame on the bottom of page 116. I have attempted to show a variety of frames. There was definitely some hand work on each piece. Even if they originally did, most no longer have glass. Some have gently domed pieces of glass. I'm sure you know that the large oval glass frames are very expensive and mostly unavailable so it follows that any frames with curved or domed glass would be much more expensive. My frames contain treasured pictures of treasured ancestors — to total strangers whose pictures came with the frame. Seemed like that was where they belonged. $2.00 – $35.00.

This piece was purchased in British Columbia. It is marked France. The easel on back of the medallion is made of brass. $65.00.

117

SEWING TOOLS

Pincushions. What a diverse selection! Different shapes and sizes. Different mate
als used to make the cover for the actual pincushion. Some of the padded domes l
off to reveal a space to store other items related to sewing. $10.00 – 18.00. This pi
ture also includes other handicraft items and tools. In the lower left corner are tw
tatting shuttles. The bobbin inside the shuttle holds a fine thread that is tied in
series of knots to create a design that can be used as an edge on collars, handke
chiefs, or lend a bit of frill to the front of a frock. The intricate and usually rap
hand movements look like an act of magic as the thread slips through the open er
of the shuttle or between the shuttle and finger as the shuttle is passed through
loop to tie a series of knots.

Front, left to right
Tatting shuttles. $4.00 – 8.00.
Knitting needles. $3.00.
Crochet hook, awl, thread cutter. $2.00 – 5.00 each.

Scissors. $5.00 – 8.00.
Thimble. $3.00 – 5.00.
Tape measure. $12.00 – 28.0

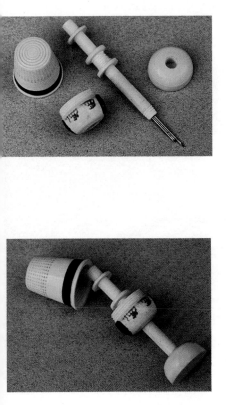

The miniature sewing kit.
$125.00 – 165.00.

A tatting case with shuttle
and two tools. $32.00 –
45.00.

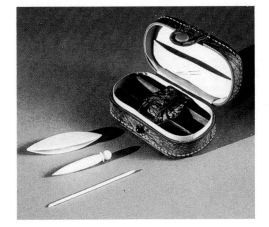

SHAVING EQUIPMENT

Back row, left to right:

        Powder shaker, with lid. $8.00 – 18.00.

        Folding mirror with shaving bowl, one brush. $35.00 – 60.00.

        Shaving brushes. $3.00 – 8.00 each.

        Hat brush. $20.00 – 25.00.

Left side:

        Die (one of a pair of dice). $6.00 – 7.50.

        Knife (metal and manufacturing cause price variations). $6.00 – 30.00.

        Shoehorn, standard. $3.00 – 6.00.

        Scratcher. $6.00 – 12.00.

Middle row, left to right:

        Soap box. $3.00 – 6.00.

        Razor, straight. $8.00 – 25.00.

        Razor, duplex. $8.00 – 12.50.

Front row, left to right:

        Comb. $8.00 – 10.00.

        Tweezers. $5.00 – 6.00.

        Blemish squeezer. $3.00 – 5.00.

        Corn knife. $45.00.

        Double (matching) brushes, men's. $12.00 – 18.00.

Beginning on the left side of the back row of this picture you will see two upright containers for loose powder. One has a disk attached to the top that can be rotated to close the holes. The other container has holes punched in a star shape. What care or detail to have these extra little touches of beauty!

The largest object in this picture is a folding shaving set. The mirror folds over the shaving bowl to make a very compact unit. I have seen six-sided powder containers that are made to fit the spaces on each side of the mirror. There is another box, similar to a powder box to the left and the natural bristle brush to the right of the glass soap dish. There were two identical units in the show where I first saw this piece. I have seen one since.)

Each shaving brush is unique. Each is marked "sterilized." That always amuses me as it is something we take for granted in our present world. The brush on the right could be for brushing off a just shaved neck or a beaver hat, as I was told when I purchased it. Although soft, the animal hairs of which this brush is made, are stiff enough for it to stand alone.

Beginning again at the left side is a single die made in HongKong. Next, a folding pocket knife, a shoehorn, and a scratcher with a slot which I suspect might have been used to hold it in a fitted case.

Middle row, left to right: The soap box holder is probably one of the items most familiar to the general public next to the powder or puff box. This one is typical with a simple rectangular box with a slightly larger top. There is a half circle removed from the edge of the top on each side to more easily lift off the lid. This box would hold a bar of wet soap and keep it from dripping on everything else.

An assortment of duplex and straight razors. I hear rumors that there is a resurgence of use of the straight razor and they are becoming less visible at shows and shops.

The two-piece celluloid box with pressed "Durham-Duplex" and an intricate scene with flags, on the outside of the upper lid. The inside of the lid has a cross-piece of celluloid which stores the double blade unit which clips into the holder for use. The holder shaft reads: "Pat. U.S.A. May 28, 07. and Foreign Countries."

The blade unit has two pieces. They must be put onto the handle together as only the guard has clips. One is a double-edged blade and the other is a series of "teeth" or blunt divisions which would act as a guard and assist in cutting and shaping sideburns and mustaches.

In the red cardboard "Durham-Duplex" box which reads: "The Blades Men Swear By — Not At. Durham Duplex Razor Co., No. 20 Jersey City - Sheffield - Paris - Toronto."

This razor shaft is marked: "Pat. U.S.A. Nov. 7, 11 and Foreign Countries." The double razor blade also has the date "Nov. 7, 191 U.S.A." and can only be attached by the toothed guard holding it in place.

These particular Durham-Duplex razors were purchased for $6.50 to $15.00. Often I see straight razors marked to $35.00. They are still in demand and use — sharpened frequently with razor strop.

Behind the comb in the front row, are several small items. You can see them more closely in other places in this book: page 83 will show you the tweezers from a side view. The double-ended tool is on page 84. The corn knife is shown on page 124.

The matching hair brushes are typically called men's double hair brushes. They are used by placing one in each hand and simultaneously brushing backward on each side of the head. Can't you see this action taking place as a suave, debonair male admires himself in the mirror?

SPECIAL TOOLS

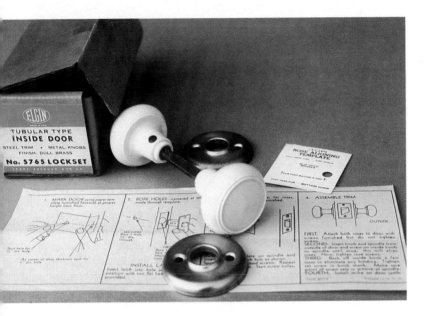

Door Knob. $15.00 – 35.00.
How excited I was to find this set complete with box, instructions, and brass hardware! It also has a template or installation guide. Purchased for $15.00.

Compass. $6.00 – 12.00.
This compass has a short hollow handle that fits very well over a wooden pencil. The reverse side has a signalling mirror — perfect for when you have gotten lost because you didn't really know how to use the compass! There is a slot in one side of the handle of the compass. It is about an inch long. I'm sure it had a special use! An old sea captain I know suggested that it might have fit over a clip or knob to prevent it from twisting about.

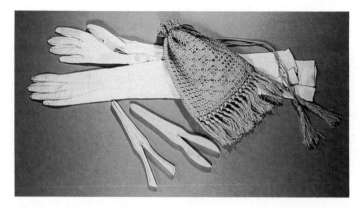

Glove Stretcher. $24.00 – 45.00.
This is used to shape the leather glove while it is drying. No doubt white leather gloves needed more than an occasional laundering and this tool would be inserted into the fingers so that the leather did not stick stiffly together as it dried. This special tool would be used to pinch and pull and stretch to return the leather to a suppleness necessary for a good fit to such a vital piece of clothing for the proper young lady. And what delicate tiny hands! The photo includes a pair of very long gloves and a draw-string crocheted purse as well as two pair of glove stretchers of different patterns.

Assorted knives. Individual knives are often available at $6.00 to 8.00 or more depending on the quality of the metal used for the blade. Folding or jackknife. $6.00 – 8.00. Corn knife. $45.00. Folding knife on a chain. $10.00. "Razor-nife" JOHN T. CARSON OIL CO. $6.00. Two-blade jackknife. $15.00.

Guy Rule. A tool consisting of double revolving circles on a 3½" base for AT & T Co. employees to calculate safely guying wires on a telephone pole. It has Patent 1,429,264. It is used in a manner similar to using a slide rule which are sometimes presented in the round as well as ruler shape. It is in perfect condition with every word readable in black and red letters and all three layers of circles rotate smoothly. Museum quality. $125.00 – 150.00.

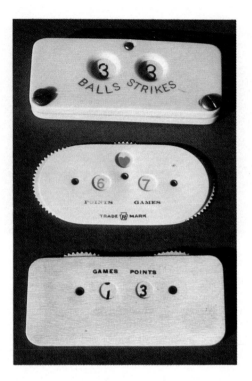

Scorekeepers. I am told that baseball umpires in the present day hold a small calc
lator or scorekeeper in their right hand while their left hand is devoted to manua
keeping track of runs in or was it foul balls? Until I was told this, it had not occurr
to me that this might have been used by an umpire. There are two thick rectang
approximately 1¼" wide by 3" long. Each is nearly ⅛th inch thick. As you can see
is held together by two large and one small brass screws which screw directly ir
the lower plate. It has two round windows to reveal Balls (up to 4) and Strikes (up
3) with two revolving disks. The letters and numbers are deeply excised and paint
black for good visibility. It shows very little wear — must not have been used in ve
exciting games. I have always thought it was made of celluloid. Now on closer eva
ation I must admit that it isn't really eligible to be in my celluloid collection —
believe it is made of ivory, but I did wish to share it with you. The scorekeeper
the center is an oval made of two layers of very thin celluloid with three tooth
disks held so they may be rotated to reveal:
1. The basic four card suits — clubs, diamonds, hearts, and spades
2. Points to 9
3. Games to 9
The lower edge says: "Trade R (in modified jar shape) Mark" The lower scorekee
er is rectangular shaped with slightly rounded corners. It has only two wheels
Points and Games up to 9. I am not sure what game it would be used to keep sco
This cost me $3.00 some years ago. $6.00 – 15.00.

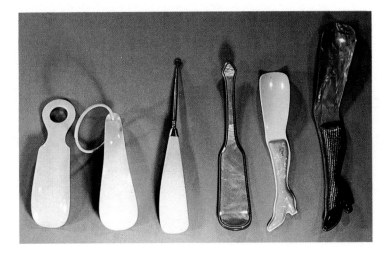

Shoehorns. $3.00 – 18.00. A very simple straight-forward tool that is used in the present day! The only one of the group that might not be used at present is the one near the center which is a combination shoehorn and button hook — that is unless you have high top shoes that have buttons! Come to think of it, I have seen this type of shoe being worn again lately. I live near a college where many of the students are into vintage clothes and perhaps they are really in need of this item to help them get to class on time.

From left to right:

1. A simple shoehorn entirely made of celluloid with a circle removed from one end — good for twirling this around your finger or hanging it on a hook somewhere convenient near to where you might put on your shoes. $5.00.

2. A simple shoehorn entirely made of celluloid with a celluloid loop. $8.00.

3. The shoehorn mentioned in the paragraph above that is half shoehorn/half buttonhook. $18.00.

4. A shoehorn made of green pearlized celluloid with black outline applied to a thicker clear amber layer. $3.00.

5. A 7" celluloid shoehorn with a puffed yellow pearlized boot-shape applied to the handle end — rather cute! $12.50.

6. A similarly shaped shoehorn with pearlized green applied to olive green plain celluloid back for the full 11" length. The applied portion is puffed bright green and metallic-striped knee stocking with back applied pump shoe. Note the strange angle. It is the perfect angle for using this shoehorn! $12.50.

TABLE ITEMS

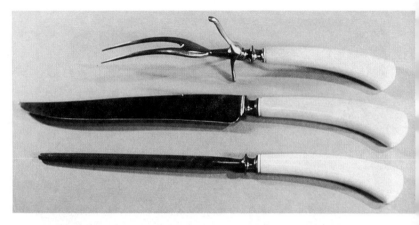

At a garage sale I found this terrific carving set for $8.50. A 15" long carving knife standing fork, and sharpening hone with matching handles. $15.00 – 35.00.

Stainless steel knife with celluloid handle, $6.00 – 8.00.
Napkin rings in assorted designs. $8.00 – 12.00 each.
The molded spoon and fork were sold as a set for $18.00. These were the only ones I have ever seen in 30 years of collecting. $25.00.

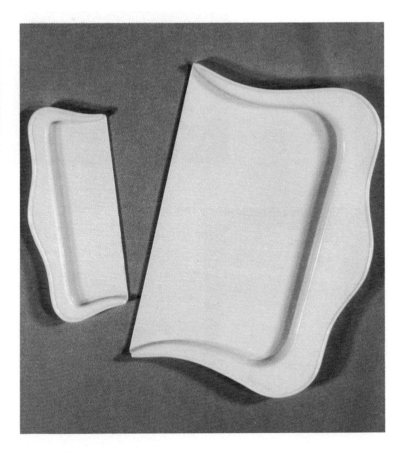

This dustpan-shaped pair is sometimes called a silent butler or crumber used to remove crumbs from a table. One is a miniature of the other. Each is of very simple one-piece construction without seams. $8.00 – 12.00 pr.

WHAT IS IT?

It looks like some kind of scratcher. Look at those sharp little teeth! About the right depth to reach deep into a beard? $6.00 – 12.00.

A temporary cast for a very small wrist? A tie holder for a very thick tie? I purchased it in a collectors mall for $6.00. $12.00 value.

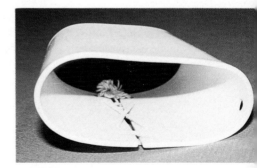

How can we possibly be sure we know exactly what an item was used for 60 to 100 years ago? It is my opinion that this was used to hang a dry bouquet in an early vintage automobile. What is your guess?

VARIATIONS

A lways, the public wants something new, something a little bit different. I'm sure that was the same with celluloid. Looking like elephant tusk ivory or Irish Belleek was just not enough after a while so improvements and modifications had to be made not just in shape and size, but in appearance and color.

To give the material variety, fish scales were added to give a pearlized look, and even later color was added for a combination of the pearlized with color (but without striations). I am told that there were 200 colors; however, I have only seen black, coral, pink, yellow, aqua, and green. Of course, there is also the amber to imitate the beautiful amber which occurs in nature but the faux does not have nature's contribution of captured insects or bits of leaves.

I have seen some truly beautiful sets looking totally new. These were priced at $145.00 to $185.00. They were not as attractive to me personally as the ivory colored.

This dresser set belonged to Margret Risley of Springfield, Pennsylvania. The purchase price was $8.50, Sears, Roebuck & Co., c. 1930s. Courtesy of Roy and Betty Barnes, Bingen, WA.

Amber and ivory set. $30.00 – 55.00.

Puff box, side view. $20.00 – 25.00.
The amber is one solid piece inside with the ivory shell
on the upper and lower half revealing the amber midway.
As you can see in the picture of the complete set above,
this piece is much more golden ivory, yet matching in
shape.

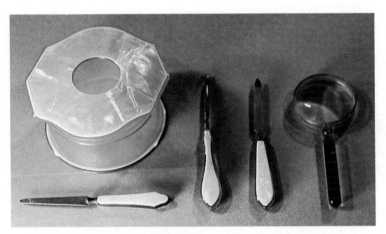

Amber and pearlized ivory receiver. $6.00 – 8.00.
Magnifying glass. $6.00 – 8.00.
Tools. $3.00 – 5.00 each.

Green puffed pearlized with decoration. $25.00 – 30.00.

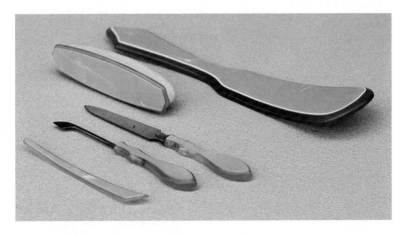

Coral pink and amber sandwich, 5 small pieces. $10.00 – 12.00.

Vanity box, side view. $18.00 – 22.00. See DuPont Catalog, page 74, Sheraton pattern of Pyralin, and page 136 in matching set.

Golden glow Pearl-on-amber set. $25.00 – 45.00.
From front clockwise:

  Perfume tray
  Shoehorn, amber only
  Button hook
  Nail file
  Polisher (buffer) with amber tray
  Hair brush, handled
  Mirrored tray
  Hand mirror
  Box with pedestal, not included in set price.

Yellow set with gold and green tulip design. $20.00 –
30.00.

Ivory with green rhinestones, compact. $12.00 – 15.00. Comb and case
(burn), gold colored rhinestones. $8.00 – 10.00.

Brush with pearlized yellow and amber/hot pink rhinestones design on top. $25.00 – 28.00.

Prices being asked for items with rhinestones are outrageous! Since I did not purchase it — I can only tell you that $79.00 firm was being asked for a folding comb of this quality and material with red rhinestones. The pieces with rhinestones are attractive and hard to find, but this brush was purchased for $3.00 in the summer 1994.

LATER PIECES

Celluloid was just the beginning!

Whether you place its origin in 1855 as Parkesine, the chloroform and cas-
r oil product of the English chemist Alexander Parkes or the outgrowth of the
rmula developed by John Wesley Hyatt as he competed for Phelan and Col-
nder's reward for a satisfactory substitute for elephant ivory to make billiard
lls, this first man-made plastic was the beginning of a giant industry of the
ture from the dresser sets and other utilitarian items for the consumer of the
e 1800s and early 1900s to the entirely different use of Hyatt's uniformly
in celluloid in photography. To many "celluloid era" meant the development
the motion picture industry.

Some events and people of this era:

George Eastman left school at 13 to support his family and while working
a bank clerk, patented a machine to coat photographic plates.

John Carbutt, a photographer, coated sheets of celluloid with an emulsion
1885 for photographing pictures.

In 1888 Eastman's first Kodak camera was loaded at the factory with cellu-
id film. When 100 photographs had been taken the camera was returned to
e factory for the film to be developed and printed. The camera was reloaded
ith film. In 1891, a new Kodak paper-backed roll of celluloid film was intro-
iced.

Both of the gentlemen mentioned above were customers of John Wesley
yatt. His ability to provide consistently thin sheets of celluloid at the Cellu-
id Mfg. Co. enabled them to replace the fragile glass plates used in photogra-
iy with celluloid, also known as Pyroxylin and cellulose nitrate. Celluloid
mained the base for all kinds of film until about 1920 when cellulose acetate
fety film began to be used and because of the safety factor it entirely
iperceded celluloid by 1955.

Leo Hendrik Baekeland invented Velox photographic paper and then in
)06, more directly related to our topic, another man made product. This one
ade entirely of inorganic chemicals: Bakelite (by an interaction of phenol and
rmaldehyde). Catalin was the name of a phenolic that could be cast, as
)posed to Bakelite which was molded.

Simultaneously other formulas were being invented and tried. DuPont
:veloped and marketed Lucite with its new crystal clear look. See 1930 – 31
talog on page 71.

These new products, corrected the disadvantages or flaws of celluloid.
:lluloid's major flaw was its extreme flammability. Plastics were developed
r specific uses. Often while one product would correct a problem, it might
ive a fault of its own such as the shape of Lumarith or cellulose acetate dis-
rting when immersed in water for any length of time.

Casein plastics were used primarily for buttons, belt buckles, and dress
ips. Urea formaldehyde was another formula for plastic. In 1929 the American

Cyanamid Corp. developed Beetle to complete the color gap into the past blue and greens and other pastel colors.

Dr. Otto Rohm developed acrylic resin and Rohm and Haas markete methyl and ethylesters with the catalyst benzoyl peroxide. This gave the cor sumer the ability to repair or design and produce plastic or epoxy items. Th creative person was no longer limited to decorating with decals and dribbles paint.

This is a condensed version of the history of various plastics. I apologize the talented individuals who were responsible for the development of th many industries that make our lives easier as well as more interesting. I valu their talent and contributions.

Look around you at the plastics in your life. Ponder the steps that brough this product to you and me. Contemplate the myriad of items being designe and produced daily for generations of new collectors. The fascination continue

Silhouette on celluloid. $9.00 – 12.00.
A design of a lady in graceful full-length bouffant dress is painted or printed on a curved surface of clear celluloid. This is similar to the pictures painted only in black on the inside of a glass surface and usually with colorful picture backgrounds in the inside back of the frame. This frame is a heavier black celluoid.

ottie dog in a black hat. $8.00 – 10.00.
tis is not just any old Scottie dog —
s is a representation of Fala, the first
g — a gift to our 32nd president from
cousin Margaret Suckley. Fala was a
nstant companion surviving his master,
anklin Delano Roosevelt, who died
ril 12, 1945. During his years in the
nite House, Fala became a favorite of
nation. He was portrayed not only in
early plastics but in mechanical tin
ys, plaster statues, ironwork, and glass
ters, candy containers, and cream
chers. *The White House and its Thirty-
ee Families* by Amy La Follette Jensen,
pyright 1958, 1962 McGraw-Hill.

Mickey Mouse. $9.00 – 12.00.
Brain child of Walt Disney in his first animated cartoon called
"Steamboat Willie" released in 1928, this one-dimensional
piece cut from a flat piece of ⅛" thick celluloid has been painted with red and black and attached to a black oval base to hold
it upright.

Magician's hat. $32.00 – 35.00.
There sits the shiny black top hat with a gentlemen's white gloves on the rim.
As the gloves are moved slightly, up pops the rabbit!